THE PIMPS RULED BY FEAR

The girls were afraid to break away from the streets, afraid they would be found, tortured and killed. The captain showed Al pictures of the victims. No training at the Police Academy had prepared him for the cumulative effect of so many horrifying deaths. He swallowed with difficulty as the captain laid out another pair of pictures. It was hard to imagine that the pretty blonde girl graduating from junior high was the same girl lying in a ditch, maggots crawling on her hairless skull . . .

"There has to be a place where working girls can go to get away from their pimps," the Captain said.

"Exactly what I had in mind," Al replied. "Midwest Challenge."

Later that night as he worked on plans to open a Safe House for prostitutes, the phone rang. A woman's voice asked if he was the man promising to protect hassled whores. Al said "yes," but he wondered. Was the woman being coached by her pimp? Was his plan to be scotched by a set-up before it began?

Al Palmquist's standing offer to all girls who want help *now:*

HOT LINE
TO FREEDOM
1-612 825-2469

ARE YOU HASSLED BY YOUR PIMP?
And are you ready to make a change in your life?

WE OFFER PROTECTION
And transportation to a "safe house"
in Minneapolis.

SAFE HOUSE IS THE FIRST OF ITS KIND
A Christ-centered program offering understanding, training, help and direction for a new life.

IT'S FREE! CALL US IF YOU'RE SERIOUS.
WE CARE!

THE MINNESOTA CONNECTION

AL PALMQUIST
with
JOHN STONE

WARNER BOOKS

A Warner Communications Company

WARNER BOOKS EDITION

Copyright © 1978 by Bible Voice, Inc.
All rights reserved

ISBN 0-446-90024-9

Warner Books, Inc., 75 Rockefeller Plaza, New York, N.Y. 10019

 A Warner Communications Company

Printed in the United States of America

Not associated with Warner Press, Inc., of Anderson, Indiana

First Printing: August, 1978

10 9 8 7 6 5 4 3 2 1

THE
MINNESOTA
CONNECTION

Author's Note

This is a true story written from police records, interviews with ex-prostitutes and pimps, and the personal experiences of Al Palmquist and numerous other officers of the Minneapolis Police Department.

Certain names have been changed and some backgrounds disguised in order to protect the subjects of the story from the very real threat of retaliation by the criminal elements described.

The primary purpose of this book is to expose serious problems that need to be solved. Hopefully, readers may do more than turn the pages to the end which should be a beginning.

J. S.

asked hopefully.

The detective shrugged.

We moved on to the M

Prologue

Blood splattered the entry to the emergency room as a hysterical girl struggled in the arms of a Minneapolis police officer. Nurses rushed to help.

"Rape victim?"

"Hardly. She's a hoe." The officer sighed when he saw the nurse didn't understand street language. "A hooker, a prostitute."

Screaming profanities, the girl was strapped to a stretcher and wheeled to an examining room. The officer followed close behind.

"We can handle her now," said an intern waiting to administer a hypo.

The officer shook his head. "She's a murder suspect."

The nurse who'd begun cutting away the girl's blood-soaked blouse looked up, eyes widening, "She's just a baby, barely into a training bra."

"Fourteen years old."

"My God." The intern closed his eyes for a moment—as if to lead a silent prayer—before beginning his examination.

Multiple scalp lacerations had bled into the girl's hair until it was hard to see she was blond. Her nose was smashed. The once smooth skin of her chest and back was furrowed with bleeding welts. On her abdomen were gray pits with angry red rims—cigarette burns.

The intern lowered his lids again—this time to blot a tear—and protested, "She's been tortured."

"So was the dead girl, another hoe about the same age." The officer explained that the suspect on the examining table had been found beside the body, holding the gun.

"In broken hands?" Less than a year out of medical school the intern had already seen too many casualties of the war on the streets. His voice rose angrily. "I know the game and the players. This is the work of a pimp. What happened to him?"

"He got away. Look, Doctor, if it makes you feel any better, call him the murderer and her a material witness."

"We'd all feel better if you locked up every sadistic scum in the pimping business and put an end to this slavery."

Biting his lower lip, the officer nodded slowly. In Minneapolis during the summer of 1977, there were at least 200 active pimps recruiting youngsters for a life of prostitution. Using dope, blackmail and terror, they preyed on the weak and confused, the runaways, the fatherless and the loveless. Ruling their sordid domain by fear, the pimps made horrible examples of girls who tried to break away or talked too much. That's why it was so hard to make cases against them. Witnesses were too scared or dead.

So it was with the girl being wheeled away to the operating room where surgeons might repair her broken body but never heal the scars on her mind. The filthy game would continue and the police officer, head bowed, seemed to wonder if he'd ever be more than a referee.

On the street they called her Candy. In the Hennepin County Hospital she refused to answer to any name. She cursed the sympathetic detectives who, after reading her her rights, admitted they didn't believe she was a killer. She refused to see an attorney or talk to the juvenile authorities. Three days after surgery she tried to escape, sneaking bandaged and half-naked through

11

the corridors, fighting viciously when sheriff's deputies in charge of security found her hiding under soiled sheets in the laundry room. When she threatened suicide, Candy was transferred to the psychiatric wing.

Her parent's, nameless, could not be found.

A nurse, knowing that I was a special kind of cop, called me for help.

Chapter 1

My shirt, light blue and neatly pressed when I put it on in the early morning, was much darker and plastered to my chest before noon. The traffic lights seemed longer, the temperature higher, as I drove toward the center of Minneapolis. A bus rumbled to a stop beside my car. The passengers fanned themselves with newspapers, anything to stir the air. As the light changed, I accelerated away from the exhaust fumes and leaned into the open window. Sometimes during August, 1977, I wished I was rich enough to afford air conditioning everywhere. But usually, I ignored the infernal weather, a small problem.

Pulling into a parking space near the

county hospital, I bowed my head. My job, combining careers as cop and clergyman, was always challenging and often too difficult to tackle alone. I knew I was going to need help inside.

When asked, the Lord has been with me, though at times I've wondered where and why He was leading me. Beginning when I was a teenager, my life was unsettled. Mother, an Irish Catholic with policemen perched on every branch of her family tree, insisted I should grow to enforce the law or, as the other choice, become a priest. Father, a proud Swede bred from many generations of Lutheran ministers, wanted me to preach in his church.

I was a rebel, my life's course uncharted.

Wising up soon after I first met my wife Gayle, I stepped forward at a Billy Graham Crusade and accepted God's invitation to be born again. Gayle's helped me steer the family in a Christian direction ever since. After three years of ministerial training at Bethany Fellowship in Minneapolis I began preaching. My father was proud and happy.

My mother still thought I should be a cop. Police work intrigued me, but it seemed God wanted to keep me working full time for Him.

On a trip to New York, I encountered

14

David Wilkerson, the minister who founded the famed Teen Challenge and later wrote *The Cross and the Switchblade*. After a short meeting, Dave locked his intense eyes onto mine and said, "God told me you're supposed to work here."

Gayle and I moved to New York a week later, all our belongings packed in a single suitcase. My training for work with young criminals, dope addicts and derelicts consisted of only nine words, "Go out on the street and trust the Lord."

Armed only with faith I began to learn how devious, vicious and violent people could become. And how much they needed help. My ministry with Teen Challenge lasted four and a half years on streets where every corner could lead to crime, to disaster. I wanted the chaos to stop. This desire to enforce the law grew steadily until I decided to return to Minneapolis and enter the Police Academy.

Friends accused me of running from God. To prove them wrong I became a guest preacher while training to be a cop. When I joined the force, my mother was elated but soon I began to feel guilty. I didn't feel I was helping anyone. I wanted to do more than put people in jail. I was troubled. I was confused. Gayle saw my turmoil and tried to help me. I didn't want to talk about it. My prayers were equally short, and there seemed to be no answers to the questions about my career. Gayle urged me to continue praying, asking for insight.

Finally, when it seemed I should return to Teen Challenge in New York where my police experience would enable me to better understand and help solve the problems young people faced on the streets, the phone rang. Frank Reynolds, the director of Teen Challenge in Rehrersburg, Pennsylvania, asked me to come east to head up their drug education ministry. Without hesitation, I said yes, knowing God had just confirmed my tentative decision.

Six months later, I was given the added responsibility of directing fund raising. I was a good salesman, but suddenly I was frustrated again. I really missed law enforcement. I began considering a return to Minneapolis. Nothing made sense. I was helping to build a strong and useful organization, serving the Lord, but I wanted out. I wanted to be a policeman again. Really? Or was I just another rover, unable to sustain any real effort anywhere? I began to doubt my sanity.

My mother called to say my father had suffered a heart attack. His condition was critical. I left for Minneapolis immediately, praying all the way: asking God to save my dad and to help me know my future. His answer came high above the Great Lakes; my dad would survive and the time had arrived for me to use my varied experience to develop a new and different ministry through police work.

The only problem was getting back on the force. There was a freeze on all city jobs. Frustration again. Gayle reassured me that God would work it out. There were no 'maybe's' when you dealt with the Lord.

Several weeks later the freeze on jobs was going off and I was going on the force. Give Him credit. God had overruled the city council.

City Hall continued to feel His influence. Early in 1972 I was called into the Mayor's office and given the unexpected commission of "helping drug addicts find Christ." A dedicated law enforcement agency had taught me how to function usefully on the street; a unique ghetto ministry had shown me how to supplement the law, and He had led me even as I misunderstood the direction.

Now, seven years later, I was about to expand my ministry again.

Candy was waiting behind locked doors

in the psychiatric wing. She was propped against white pillows, swathed in fresh bandages, antiseptically clean. She held her bruised lips tight together.

I introduced myself and suggested that she give me the names of her parents. "Maybe they can help you."

"Shit."

Pretending she hadn't spoken, I started to tell her about help from the Lord.

"I've been to Sunday school. Didn't like it. Look, I told the pigs yesterday, I got nothing to say. Bug off."

Being a big-boned man, well over six feet and two hundred pounds, it was easy to act intimidatingly. I guessed that's what she was accustomed to, would respond to—a menace.

Struggling to pull off the act with a four-teen-year-old girl, I leaned over the bed and growled, "Maybe we should just turn you loose and start spreading the word that you've narced on your pimp. Then maybe we can bust him for blasting *your* head off."

She recoiled, pushing deeper into her pillow. "You're just like my pimp. You're trying to game me."

That hurt. Pimps used the expression 'game' to describe the brainwashing process by which young girls are forced into prostitution. It involves total destruction of self-esteem and obliteration of all will. Successfully employed, 'gaming' brought a near Pavlovian response to any command from the sex merchants.

I admitted I was trying to psych her. "But for the Lord. He can help and He is gentle."

"Like you?"

I apologized.

Candy began to cry.

I tried again to get the names of her parents.

She shook her head. "Nobody cares."

"I care, Candy. Jesus cares."

"You're gaming me again." She shouted, but her voice chattered, sounding like she wasn't sure. She was beginning to act her age, her eyes begging for love.

"There is help for you. We're after the pimps. They're the real criminals. Do you remember from Sunday school where the Bible refers to whoremongers right along with kidnappers and murderers?"

She shook her head again, but slowly. She was beginning to relax, listening.

"It's in I Timothy. And the Bible tells too how Jesus helped prostitutes."

"But there weren't as many pimps then. If I talk to you, they'll get me. Their people are everywhere. In jail, in the juvenile home.

There's no place to be safe, just sorry." Terror returned to her darting eyes.

"I have a way." She was really young, but if there was no one else to help her. . . .

"Through Jesus Christ. Sure, but before I go to heaven my tail will get nailed to a cross."

It was hard to believe I was hearing that from a little girl. I shook my head and began telling her about Midwest Challenge, a sanctuary where ex-addicts and others with problems could begin a new life.

"I don't mainline." She held out her arm. "How'd you know I was into dope?"

"Most hookers are. Isn't that part of the game?"

Candy nodded, blinking away more tears. "So you can help people on drugs. But what about us that have pimps? I told you, they can get in anywhere."

She had a point. Helping hookers, fourteen-year-old hookers, fight off pimps was a new mission. I stopped to think. Then, flexing my muscles, I resumed a menacing posture.

"You'd be safe at Midwest Challenge because pimps are afraid of tough cops and I am a very tough cop."

"Sure." She made a small smile, wincing as it stretched the cuts at the corners of her mouth. "Let me think. Come see me to-morrow."

Our first meeting ended with a prayer. Candy didn't join me, but I hoped she was listening.

Chapter 2

Candy's case involved more than prostitution, assault and murder. She was an example of the growing trend to recruit 'chili-dog hookers' (so-called because they were very young, often seen walking the streets eating chili-dogs or popping bubble gum as they peddled their bodies).

Prostitution has always been a problem in Minneapolis, as in all large cities. The Mayor's office and the police department sought to control, if not end, the vicious game that destroyed women mentally and physically. The standard procedure was to arrest and convict the whores. But such intervention without rehabilitation accomplished little and salvaged few lives. Sentences were usually short and the women quickly returned to the streets to be reduced to hollow shells ultimately needing support from society through its welfare programs.

And now young girls, not much older than my daughter, were involved. The very idea of 'chili-dog hookers' enraged me. The reality of Candy's destructive lifestyle fired my determination that Midwest Challenge should begin helping prostitutes.

Since Midwest Challenge was interdenominational, its work already encouraged by city hall, I was sure the police chief would endorse my new efforts. Certainly, I could start by helping to solve the current murder case and aid in the war against the pimps.

I returned to the hospital early the next morning, hoping Candy would put me in touch with her parents. Then, if her homelife proved unsuitable, I planned to ask the juvenile authorities to place her in the care of Midwest Challenge.

Some people disagreed with the religious emphasis in my work. Police officers, politicians, businessmen, social workers asked, "Why shove the Bible at us? We already agree that your program is important and successful, a good work. Why cloud the issue?"

My answer: "Spiritually, because I believe we all need to find a place with the Lord, to be born again. Logically, because Midwest Challenge and its Christian approach works. Ninety-three percent of the young people completing the program continue to lead useful, law-abiding lives. This is the highest success ratio of any similar program, religious or not, in the country."

Candy was very pale, her hands twitched nervously, when I came into the room.

"You've got to get me out of here. This part of the hospital is full of weirdos. I could hear them screaming all night."

I agreed to help if she promised to behave. "And if you begin answering my questions."

Her parents were divorced. Neither lived in the state. Barely thirteen, Candy ran away from her mother, a cocktail waitress, who "maybe sold herself on the side." She hadn't heard from her father in ten years, couldn't remember what he looked like. She'd come to Minneapolis on the bus and met her pimp before leaving the bus station.

"Did you know he was a pimp?"

"No way. I wasn't even broken in yet. But he seemed to know I smoked dope, and he gave me some, and he seemed to care, really care, and . . ." She reached toward the bandages on her face and began to sob. "He said I was beautiful."

Candy lived with her pimp for three months before the gaming began. He spent a lot of money on her, convincing her they were in love, taught her to meet his every sexual need, and then suggested that she "go to work." When she refused, Candy learned that fear and pain were a large part of the street and that coat hanger whippings were a way of life for street walkers. Her pimp twisted a coat hanger so that it looked like a long wire with a hook at the end. Tearing off her expensive clothes, he beat her until she passed out, revived her and beat her again. No part of her body was spared the searing slashes of the metal, the gouges from the cruel hook.

The next day, still caked with blood, she was sent onto the streets with the admonition, "They don't have to see your body. Use your mouth."

Furious, I interrupted her story. "What's his name?"

"Please."

It hurt me to push her, even with words, but I had to know. "His name, or you'll be sleeping here tonight."

She told me in the most frightened voice I've ever heard. "Clarence Jones. 'Zip Whip' Jones."

"Where can I find him?"

She didn't know. He moved around a lot keeping track of his string of whores.

I was terribly angry, ready to tear apart the man who violated and tortured little girls, and was now a murderer. Common sense and police training kept me from rushing out to search for him. I needed to know the rest of the story first.

Candy would usually go to work about 9:00 p.m. and stay on the streets until after 4:00 a.m. Turning as many tricks (the prostitutes' term for a sexual encounter) as possible, she'd return exhausted to her pad and give all the money to Zip Whip.

"I go $25, sometimes $50, a trick. I earned maybe $200 on a good night."

She said it proudly, but lowered her eyes when she saw me frowning sadly.

"Sometimes after a night of turning tricks, Zip would make love to me. He said he wanted to make me feel like a real woman. Off and on he'd bring another one of his girls over and the three of us would do it together. Sort of like practice for special parties."

I cocked an eyebrow. Was she into group sex too?

"Everything. The night it happened, the killing I mean, I'd already had a really bad, crazy scene with a john." She took a deep breath. "That's what we call customers."

"I know." I wanted to add that the johns were as guilty as the pimps, but she kept talking faster and faster, as if she wanted to finish the sex scene quickly.

"I was working a convention in a downtown hotel when I noticed a sweet looking man about fifty. He had grey hair and was very dignified in a blue vested suit. I cuddled up to him and asked about a date. He knew what I meant and took me straight to his room. When the door was locked he offered a hundred bucks if I let him tie me up naked to the old-fashioned bed post. 'No sex, just let me look.' How easy can it get? I thought. The easiest hundred I ever earned." She shuddered.

I reached to take her hand, worried she would aggravate her wounds.

"After about ten minutes of standing naked tied to the bed post with the old man staring at me, I began to worry. His eyes got wild. Then he took off his belt and went bananas. He hit me so many times I passed out. When I woke up later I was hurting so bad that I could hardly move. I couldn't see at first because my eyes were swollen shut. When I finally found my money there was two big bills instead of one."

She saw the question in my eyes.

"No, it wasn't worth it. I could hardly get myself home. Everytime I moved I could feel the cuts open up and blood soak into my clothes, my good clothes." She began to cry.

It became harder to control my anger. I'd seen a lot of depravity and violence riding in a squad car and I'd heard about even worse. But I'd never heard such horror described by such a pathetic figure. Candy clutched me with one small hand, squeezing her pillow with the other. Her quivering body filled less than a quarter of the narrow hospital bed. Her voice was getting weaker.

"Zip was waiting with the other girl, the one that got killed, when I got home. They figured on a three-way party but when they saw me they told me to get cleaned up first. I went into the bedroom and passed out again. I had terrible nightmares. One seemed so real that I thought it was Zip and the other girl shouting at each other. She said she wanted out. She was cussing and screaming and crying all at one time, so loud that I couldn't understand everything. Just 'leave me alone, leave me alone.' Then Zip went into a real rage. 'OK bitch, you've had it. You want out? I'll let you out.' And I heard a booming noise."

"Gunshots?"

She nodded. "I ran through the living room. I shouldn't have, but I was trying to get away. Zip caught me and began beating me. I promised him I wouldn't tell. He wouldn't listen. He kept on hitting me, shouting, 'You'll get more of this and the same as her if you do.' He didn't stop until the sirens scared him off. When your people came, I was numb. I couldn't feel anything anymore. I couldn't even cry. I don't remember much after that."

"You've remembered plenty and told me about it better than most older people could." I was speaking through clenched teeth, anxious to end the interview and rush out to search for Zip Whip.

There was no record of him at police headquarters. Pimps were rarely arrested unless they broke other laws. No one on the street admitted knowing him. One informant told me that 'Zip Whip' was a favorite nickname among pimps and reminded me that 'Clarence Jones' was a common alias.

Was Candy conning me, using fake names to protect the pimp who'd threatened to kill her too?

"No way," she insisted the next morning. "It's so neat, the way you can be so hard gently. You really care."

Suddenly there was an edge on her voice and, even through the bandages, I saw her face tighten. "But you can't help me. I've thought about Midwest Challenge and I don't want to go there. I'm not good enough. I'll never be good enough."

Starting to tell her how God would give anyone the chance for a new life, I realized her emotional wounds were festering, the pus clouding her mind. Better to let her rest and heal from the traumatic disclosures of the day before.

"I'll come back tomorrow." I left a Bible with her.

Candy refused to see me again. She was released in the custody of distant relatives. Later, I learned she ran away from them too and disappeared.

Chapter 3

Worrying that I might fail with other girls like Candy, I began to study the prostitution problem in Minneapolis and discovered it was worse than most people knew or admitted. Pimps were everywhere, recruiting hundreds of teenagers every year. It was as easy to buy live sex as printed pornography. The streets and bars on Hennepin Avenue between Fourth and Tenth were crowded with hookers every night. Nicollet Avenue was infested with commercial sex. Previously, most of the hookers had appeared to me to be just girls out for a good time. Most seemed too young to be unsupervised in such a seedy environment, yet I would never have guessed so many were professionals. Now, with the help of the vice squad, I learned how to spot them.

Their cheeks were usually sunken, their eyes emotionless. Obviously, they wore too much makeup and revealing or enticing clothes. But the real givaway was their slow gait, the aimless path they followed. Pimps were always present, sulking in doorways or cruising in garish cars.

The city administration tried to discourage them. Police files were full of arrest records, mostly women with a long history of vice-related crime. The younger girls, usually runaways, were turned over to the juvenile authorities for return to their parents or placement in a foster home. There was scant evidence of preventive or rehabilitative work.

Pimps who moonlighted as drug dealers or robbers were sent to prison. Others, not needing to supplement the income of their girls, were seldom picked up.

"It's hard to make a case. You can't arrest a man for just talking or walking with a girl," said a Captain who'd been trying to eliminate prostitution for many years. "And the girls won't talk. As a matter of fact, it's nearly impossible to break up their relationships with pimps. I've tried, even taken some into my home."

He suggested we talk further "over a beer."

"Make it a soda. Remember, I'm a minister."

His smile was short. He really meant business when it came to cleaning up prostitution. Explaining that the average longevity in street prostitution is five years, he called it "the deadliest game in town" and promised to produce pictures to prove the point. He'd talked with hundreds of streetwalkers and found that a girl entering the world's oldest profession at age sixteen would be destroyed mentally, her mind not capable of normal thought patterns, by the time she was twenty-one. Physically, she'd be without feeling and probably ridden with venereal disease. Medical research indicated that four out of five women carrying VD didn't recognize any symptoms until it was too late to prevent sterility or tissue damage. Worse yet, they unknowingly passed it on.

I thought about the johns, many family men, who spread the disease to their families or other girls.

The Captain read my mind. "Sure the customer suffers when he catches a dose, but that's not punishment enough. We need stricter laws that not only allow for the arrest and conviction of those who perpetrate prostitution, but also the men who utilize prostitutes."

"What about the pimps?"

"They're slippery devils. Best way to put them out of business is to stop the supply of new girls, rehabilitate the old ones, and dry up the demand for commercial sex."

I frowned. A tough assignment. I believed I could help some girls, stop them on the way to the street or take them off. But re-educating men willing to pay anything for sex—that sounded like tilting windmills. Unless they became Christians. I smiled.

The Captain continued. "New laws may make it less attractive for men to seek out prostitutes. Education, especially of parents, will help keep many girls at home. But, if we're to clean the Minneapolis streets, there has to be a place where working girls can go to get away from their pimps."

"Exactly what I had in mind. Midwest Challenge."

"I hope you know what you're getting into."

"I'm going to try anyway."

"As far as the pimps are concerned, the best place for them is behind bars. You can help there too, if you find girls that will talk and testify."

"Damn right."

Noticing my hatefulness, he asked, "Is that a Christian attitude."

I apologized, not caring if he was kidding, and admitted I'd help pimps too, "if they really wanted to begin a new life. But I'd watch 'em close, real close."

Twenty minutes later, I was ready to strangle them all. Commenting that six percent of all Minneapolis homicides could be attributed to prostitution, the Captain showed me pictures of the victims. No training at the Police Academy, no experience on patrol, had prepared me for the cumulative effect of so many horrifying deaths. I swallowed hard as he laid out pictures of girls in acid baths, disemboweled, beaten pulpy with tire irons, doused in gasoline and burned to blackened bones. He laid their school pictures alongside. It was hard to imagine the pretty blond girl graduating from junior high was later found in a ditch, maggots crawling on her hairless skull.

No wonder Candy had been afraid to break away to a new life. Had I been younger, I might have run and hid too.

Later that night, as I was working on plans to quickly open a haven for prostitutes, the phone rang in my office at Midwest Challenge. A syrupy voice asked if I was the man promising to protect hassled hoes.

37

I answered, "Yes," but without enthusiasm. The woman's words were too carefully spoken. Was she being coached by her pimp, trying to set me up? I reached into my briefcase and fingered my 357 magnum revolver. Hey, I thought, you're supposed to be a tough cop and you know you've got the Lord on your side.

Chapter 4

Her name was Lynn and she wasn't setting me up.

"Candy told me about you before she skipped. Said you were kinda strange, but really a good guy, and with enough clout to help me."

"I'll try." I invited her to Midwest Challenge.

"Not yet, not now, not. . . . I mean my pimp's still in town. You'll have to meet me somewhere, pretend you're a john."

We met at a back booth in the bar of an expensive motel near the airport. The waitress winked at Lynn when I sat down.

"This is my regular territory. Act like you're a live one." She moved closer to me.

I shook my head. "This place is no good. I'm usually recognized as a cop or," I paused for emphasis, "a minister of the gospel."

"Some of them pay for it, just like the rest." She raised an eyebrow.

"Get it together, Lynn. Quit being flaky. You said you needed help."

"But I don't really know how to ask." She fidgeted, twisting and squeezing her hands. "I'm not used to talking to guys like you."

Certain she would never be comfortable talking to me where she worked, I suggested a restaurant on the other side of town. I flicked my eyes toward the waitress. "Don't worry. She'll think we're going to my room."

Lynn was twenty years old. She looked over thirty. The story of her life before prostitution brought tears to her eyes—and surprised me. She came from an upper middle-class Minnesota family. As a child she'd regularly attended Sunday school, was confirmed and joined a teen group at church. Always, her father bought her anything and everything she wanted. Her mother rarely criticized and never punished any of the children. Nonetheless, Lynn had been a "pretty good" little girl. Spoiled perhaps, living in a cocoon of affluence, but surely with no obvious reason to begin selling her body.

"Then why?" I was honestly confused.

"I felt rejected."

"You had a brother and a sister. Was one the favorite?"

"Not really. We all got pretty much our own way."

"Your parents had domestic problems?"

"Not until a few years ago. Then they got divorced. But I was already on the streets." She ran her tongue around her mouth, thinking. "I guess they were too much into themselves. Like dad said, 'I'll buy you anything you want, just don't ask for my time.' And I can remember, just before I set off on my own, I wanted to tell him to take his eyes off himself and look at me."

Lynn was straight, a virgin, until she was fifteen. Even later, she didn't consider herself promiscuous. She was gamed into prostitution without realizing it. Her dad bought her a house as a high school graduation present. She already had an expensive new car. Living high and alone, she began dating a young executive with a large national company. And she fell in love.

"He pretended to love me and it was glorious. Then, one day he asked me to prove I loved him, help him in his business. I said, 'sure, anything,' and he took me at my word. He sent me on a date with a man doing a deal with him. 'Be nice so it'll be a *good* deal for me,' he said. My boyfriend, the guy I loved, told me to go out and have sex with other men." She laughed sadly. "I wasn't a real whore yet. Still, I felt like one. I told him he was acting like a pimp. But he said, 'No,' and started in on the love thing and . . . oh God, how I wanted to be loved. So I began letting his business associates into me." She held out her hands, palms up. "That's how I got started—as an unpaid corporate hooker paid in love."

"Love? Your boyfriend was a pimp from the start. Did other girls work for him? What's his name? What company did he work for?" This was a new angle, something I hadn't known about. The question shot out of my mouth.

She stood up from the table. "Yes, he became my pimp, a real pimp, but he isn't now. He gave me to someone else. That's all I'm going to say until I know you better. Now take me back where we met. On the way you can tell me about this deal of yours, Midwest . . . whatever."

Walking to the car Lynn stopped, tugging at my arm like a child.

"Look, we've been talking more than two hours. You'll have to give me something. Otherwise I'll be in big trouble."

I knew what she meant. It was nearly bar time, too late to pick up good customers. She had to take money home. A lot of money. I rummaged in my pockets.

"I haven't much."

She started to giggle. "Forget it. I was dumb to ask. I've got a stash. I'll use some of that."

It began to rain. I drove slowly, wondering how to begin telling Lynn about the new program at Midwest Challenge. She seemed so ready to listen. Yet I was worried that, like Candy, she'd reject my offer and run.

Lynn lit a cigarette. I started to tell her there was no smoking in my car or at Midwest Challenge, but said only, "That's a great way to ruin your lungs."

"Why not? I guess I've wrecked everything else."

"Not beyond repair." I turned toward her, hoping she could see my smile in the dim light. I quoted from II Corinthians: "If any man be in Christ he is a new creation: old things are passed away, all things have become new."

"Is that what your program is all about?" She tossed the cigarette out the window.

"Yes. The goal of Midwest Challenge is to provide a smooth re-entry into society for anyone willing to try. Up to now, we've helped mostly ex-addicts. I hope you'll become the first ex-prostitute."

The traffic light ahead turned red and I skidded to a stop.

"For a cop, you're not the greatest driver."

We both laughed. Then Lynn turned serious, pronouncing her words carefully.

"I've always believed in God, even when I was hooking."

My eyes darted between her and the road. She'd said 'was.' Did that mean she'd already made a decision? I decided to take a chance. "When can you move into Midwest Challenge?"

"Next week. As soon as my pimp goes to New York."

"Praise the Lord."

"You really mean that, don't you?" Her voice was high and happy. She wanted to know more about Midwest Challenge.

I described how a new lifestyle was established as residents of self-sufficient houses passed through three phases of re-development, all highly structured, all requiring strict adherence to a moral code dictated by the Bible. But in safety and serenity.

When I told her the sexes were separated except during Bible class and certain work projects, Lynn interrupted, teasing, "Good idea, especially with me in the program."

Clearing my throat, I continued. "Phase one involves the Bible classes, live-in counseling, vocational training, recreation and therapy." I turned to look at her. "And tight discipline."

She didn't flinch. It seemed so many young people, especially those at Midwest Challenge, quickly learned to equate fair discipline, however strict, with love.

"Phase two continues the classes and vocational training, allows the assumption of some responsibilities along with extended freedom, provides more recreation, and . . ."

"More discipline."

"Sounds like you think you need it."

"Damn right. Oops!" She giggled. "See."

I nodded, explaining that Midwest Challenge was not a reform school or a prison. It was run by the love of Jesus. In phase three, residents received specialized vocational training and were found good jobs, often in businesses run by Midwest Challenge.

"You're kidding. What kind of businesses?"

"A coffee house, a mailing service, a manufacturing company, and Midwest Challenge itself. That's our most important business. Maybe you could work in our office."

"You're the damnest cop I've ever met." She inhaled quickly. "Wow! There I go again."

I chuckled. "If swearing and smoking are

the only bad habits you have to break now that you're coming off the street, redemption is going to be easy."

My wife was waiting up when I got home. I couldn't resist kidding her.

"Wonder why I'm so late? I've been out with a not too bad looking hooker."

"I can tell by the look on your face that she's about to become an ex-hooker. Now we've got to hurry and get a place ready for these girls. What are you going to call it?"

"Safe House."

She liked the name.

Lynn liked it too. But, when she moved in a week later she reminded me that a name was only good if it meant what it said. She was worried about her pimp.

"He'll be back from New York soon."

That was an opening to learn more about how pimps operated. "What's he doing in New York?"

Lynn hesitated.

"Look, I can't give you my best help, complete protection, unless I know what I'm up against."

"He's delivering girls."

Lynn's revelation made me nearly as furious as the time I'd seen the pictures of the slaughtered girls. Now it seemed others, preferably blonds, were being hauled across the country to be sold in a market called

'The Minnesota Strip,' the long, sin-soaked blocks that ran off Times Square along 8th Avenue. I remembered the area from when I'd worked with Teen Challenge, but I'd never guessed that many of the girls were imported from my home state.

I called the Captain. "What do you know about a pipeline feeding hookers to New York?"

He estimated that over a thousand girls between the ages of twelve and twenty-one had been funneled from the Midwest to the streets of New York in recent years. Many were from Minnesota because eastern johns preferred Scandinavian blonds. Most were never heard from again.

"I'm going to plug that pipeline!" I shouted into the phone.

"You're kidding. How? Remember Al, you're just a Minneapolis policeman. The New York department and the Federal boys haven't been able to crack it."

"Maybe they haven't tried. I don't know but, damnit, I'm going to try."

"Take it easy, Reverend."

I shook my head. The phone banged against my ear. "I won't take it easy. I want help. I'm going to get help. And, if I can't plug it, I'm going to bust the Minnesota pipeline wide open."

Chapter 5

The Mayor and the Police Chief approved of my crusade. The board of directors of Midwest Challenge, which had already agreed to help local girls, encouraged me to try saving teenage prostitutes from the Minnesota Strip in New York as well. But first, there was a matter of priorities. Safe House was almost operational, though nearly empty. Lynn was attempting to recruit for the program and needed me to support and protect her. Candy was wandering the streets somewhere, still requiring help. The regular residents of Midwest Challenge could not be neglected. The staff sought my guidance.

I called them together and explained my mission: to search and expose, rescue and restore. We prayed for God's fortification. Everyone agreed that the war against prostitution should be fought on all feasible fronts.

"The Minnesota connection with New York must be broken," said one associate. He called it "white slavery" and observed that "the world's oldest profession" was fast becoming "the world's youngest profession next to babysitting."

Working quickly, usually long into the night, often with the help of the Captain and other policemen, I developed a picture of prostitution as it exists in Minneapolis and most other large cities. Street hookers, the girls walking the pavement and soliciting in the bars, conduct seventy-five percent of the business. These are usually the ones shipped to New York. Saunas, rap parlors, escort services, call girls and corporate whores make up the remainder of the bodies for sale. Contrary to the *Happy Hooker* fallacy, the average prostitute is an unwilling participant in the lousy game. Trapped, forced and threatened with torture or death, she has little chance to escape.

"We're going to offer that chance and more," I began telling everyone.

Many thought I was promising the impossible. Some called me "an overzealous nut." Others said it was none of their business. They didn't want to get involved in anything so dirty. However, enough people realized something had to be done. It never occurred to me to be discouraged. But I was often disgusted and horrified, growing angrier by the minute.

The Captain produced case histories from police files. Prostitutes came from a wide variety of backgrounds. The one thing they had in common was that they were turned on to their business by men. Motherly madams of yesteryear seemed to have disappeared in an evolutionary process whereby fathers, lovers, husbands and pimps had become the mold makers who formed prostitutes. The process was brutal.

Ellen, raised in Saint Louis Park, Minnesota, turned fourteen during July 1974. She ran away from a domineering and overly protective father a month later. Finding herself in downtown Minneapolis with no money and no place to go, she wandered aimlessly until approached by a well-dressed young man. He offered her lunch and later marijuana. Falsely secure when high, she told him her life story, described her unhappiness. When he offered to put her up for the night, she accepted, believing he was truly concerned and close enough to her age to understand her problems. The gaming began. Compromised by marijuana and liquor, she had intercourse with him. He was gentle.

She enjoyed it. She felt safe, momentarily serene, free of worries.

The next morning the pimp, Raleigh, introduced Ellen to another girl a few years her senior. He said she was a teacher, not bothering to explain what Ellen was expected to learn.

Beginning with a lurid description of the traditional coat hanger whippings that followed disobedience, the older girl instructed Ellen how to please a man quickly, how much to charge and who got the money. The lesson ended with techniques for avoiding the police and a warning not to talk if she was caught. Her job began immediately.

Trapped by fear, too young to resist, Ellen worked alongside her instructor for five days. On the sixth day, because through inexperience she'd earned only $150, Raleigh pulled Ellen off the street and took her to an apartment in North Minneapolis. For more education, he said. Ten others were present to witness the lesson. The pimp and another whore ripped off her clothes and made her stand in a tub of water. They shocked her with an electric cattle prod and beat her with coat hangers. Later, they doused her with more water and poured salt over her body. The onlookers cheered as the whipping continued, more painful than before as the stinging salt was forced into the wounds.

When the group got too high and drunk to stop her, Ellen escaped and went to the police. Photos were taken of her injuries but corroborating witnesses were impossible to find. The County Attorney could not build a case.

Barbara, fifteen in May 1976, ran away from a fatherless home in Brooklyn Center, Minneapolis. She was picked up on the Minneapolis streets by Raleigh, the same pimp, and fed chocolate mescaline. Taken to a hotel, she was shown polaroid pictures of Ellen's punishment and threatened with the same if she did not submit to abnormal and group sex.

Later the same night, she was to be taken to the apartment in North Minneapolis and, at the point of a gun, forced to endure anal sex with a succession of men.

Barbara also escaped and went to the police. But with no witnesses, there was no prosecution.

"What about for rape?" I asked. "For abduction?"

There were no answers.

Grace came to Minneapolis on a church exchange program. While she was waiting at the depot for the bus taking her home to Goodrich, Minnesota, she met a fast talking man named Lionel. He wondered why a "good looking chick" wanted to waste herself in the boonies. Grace, only sixteen, didn't have an answer. Nonetheless, she boarded the bus, but only after giving Lionel her address and phone number. He began writing and calling, promising a really good life together.

There were problems at school; truancy and poor grades. With parents who were only strict, never communicative, Grace decided to accept Lionel's offer.

When the pimp met the bus she told him he was a better man than her father who never said anything except, "You make me ashamed."

Before leaving home, Grace had withdrawn her savings from the bank. Lionel took the $130, promising to safeguard it. Several days later, needing money for toilet articles, she asked for $10. Lionel laughed and told her she'd been a virgin long enough. The gaming started without drugs or liquor. When he raped her, Lionel discovered Grace had a low pain threshold. After that, the mere mention of physical abuse was sufficient to make her perform. She was taught to be an expert in oral sex which brought a better price from many johns.

During her first two weeks on the street, Grace earned enough money to keep Lionel happy. Then she had a slow day and received her first coat hanger whipping.

Crazed with pain, she ran half dressed to a phone booth and managed to call an uncle before her pimp caught up.

The police arrived in time to save her. Lionel was charged with three felonies, pleaded guilty to reduced charges and was back in business after serving just four months in the county jail. Later, he expanded his territory to include the Minnesota Strip in New York City. Grace was returned to her parents who finally sought professional counseling. Now, with a much wiser father, she was still scarred but learning to live a happier, wholesome life.

Many of the girls with records came from impoverished homes or family units with weak, thoughtless fathers—or no father at all. There seemed to be little love shown. Rarely, did they remember being closely held or told they were loved. When they looked elsewhere and were involved in early sexual encounters their home life deteriorated further. Most weak fathers, finding out about their daughter's sexual experiments, retaliated by threatening further deprivation of love and accused the girls of being sluts. They fired hurtful questions and undeserved accusations that were really not meant. But, because many fathers were themselves frightened and insecure, they said the very things that drove their daughters away, into the waiting arms of the pimps.

Most girls never returned, were never found. The clandestine nature and fluidity of the runaway system made it terribly difficult to track the thousands that moved through Minneapolis, let alone the rest of the country.

Cheryl was an exception. In 1973 she was seventeen and had borne an illegitimate child. She was street wise, but not wise enough. She met a man named Joey who claimed to be a part owner of *Highlife* magazine. He offered her a job dancing in Madison, Wisconsin, and said she could earn $300 a week. He invited her to his apartment but didn't suggest sex until the next day when he brought in an old man and demanded she turn a trick, "to see how good you are." She was afraid to refuse.

On the way to Madison he suggested she could earn extra money working for his friend Jack. He warned her too. Jack was a little crazy, sometimes sadistic. Apparently, Cheryl figured she could handle Jack. After meeting him, she was introduced to another of Joey's associates, Manuel Artez, who operated a sauna. The men convinced her to work as a sexual masseuse. Later, Joey returned to Minneapolis leaving orders that Cheryl should obey Jack and Manuel. They didn't bother her as long as she earned big money for them. Then police officers, following a lead that Cheryl was a runaway, raided the sauna. Jack hid her in Manuel's garage, but without proper clothing for an unheated area during a Wisconsin winter. She was locked in for nearly thirty hours, fed only one cupcake and a few cookies. Afraid she'd freeze or starve to death, Cheryl broke out and returned to Minneapolis where the police caught her.

She was tired of running and angry enough to talk. Her testimony broke an interstate vice case and helped uncover evidence that sent several pimps to prison. The exposé of the sauna where she'd worked was sufficient to scare Cheryl off the streets for good. Four other girls were involved. Three had been actually kidnapped. Two were forced to commit robberies. Several were tortured, one with a soldering iron inserted in her vagina. Cheryl admitted she was lucky and thankful.

By then, I thought I knew as much as I needed about what happened to hookers, especially 'chili-dog hookers.' Discovering exactly how the pimps operated was another matter.

Chapter 6

Every day, thousands of people passed through Crystal Court. The huge square was enclosed in the I.D.S. building, newest and tallest structure on the Minneapolis skyline. Beautifully decorated and well lit, the court was a place to eat, drink, window shop and meet friends. And, to the trained eye, it was the pimps' workshop. They wandered around the main floor, rode up and down the escalators, and lined the balconies.

I knew from police experience that this was one of the favorite places to recruit and procure whores. The others included parks, some singles bars, restaurants that stayed open late and allowed teenagers to hang around, and the bus station.

Lynn and the Captain had told me what to look for and not to be surprised if I saw more than I expected. They were right. Even though I was a police officer with many years' experience working most of the Minneapolis precincts, I'd never realized how easy it was for pimps to conduct their rotten business in such a public place.

A security guard, eyes popping with frustration because there was little he could do to discourage such activity, said recruiting went on constantly. Runaways were easily spotted. Instead of moving normally, they'd stop and start, look over their shoulders, fidget nervously with their clothes.

I spotted several immediately. Restless and paranoid, alone in a strange place, they were worried about their next meal, a bed for the night, and the police. Noticing me, they'd quickly disappear. Unfortunately, more times than not, it was the pimps ("players," the vice world called them) who spotted such girls before the police did.

It wasn't hard to see how the rest of the game was played. When pimps identified possible runaways, they'd approach with a smile and begin a simple conversation. Amazing as it seemed, a sharp player could extract the girls' life history within fifteen minutes. Pretending interest and sympathy, they became surrogate fathers. The results were no different than when insecure adults pour out their unhappy hearts to bartenders.

During these conversations, pimps determined which girls were susceptible to life as a prostitute. Unworldly backgrounds and naive desires for freedom and excitement were the tip-offs. To gain their confidence, pimps invited the prospects to parties where there was plenty of booze and pot. Such invitations served to assure the girls that the solicitous males were not connected with a law enforcement or social service agency.

Runaways, especially repeaters, feared these agencies because of past performances. They apprehended the girls and returned them immediately to the disastrous environments from which they were trying to escape. Once home, with a juvenile record, any small hope of a loving family life usually disappeared. So many girls chose to move in with pimps and learned too late that any life was better than the one on the streets.

Pimps made themselves seem attractive with fancy clothes, big cars and plush apartments. With glib tongues and fawning manners they offered escape through liquor and drugs and a form of sanctity most girls hadn't encountered before.

"Be yourself," I heard one say as he passed with a prospect clutching his arm.

"Be yourself. That's when I know I can love you."

She giggled, not knowing the pimp's kind of love meant enslavement. If I hadn't been undercover, gathering information that could end his game for good, I'd have pulled out my badge and tried to save her. I almost did, but I remembered what the Captain said. How could a policeman arrest people just for talking?

There had to be another way. With the Lord's help, any problem could be solved. I left Crystal Court determined to return one day with a solution.

Lynn rushed out to meet me when I pulled up in front of Safe House. Her cheeks were flushed, her voice squeaking with excitement. "Another girl wants to move in here."

Word of the protection we offered was beginning to spread. Safe House was working. Thank the Lord.

The new girl, Ginger, was a friend of Lynn's. Nineteen, she'd been a prostitute for three years. She'd worked in saunas and rap parlors, but mostly on the streets. She had an illegitimate child and she was trying to escape to a better life for him. Her pimp was the father. The baby was in a foster home.

"I want him back when I'm ready to be a real mother," she told me soon after arriving.

I knew that might be much later. Ginger trusted no one, hated most men. When I reached out to lead her on a welcoming tour, she jumped back. Her painful background was similar to what I'd read in the police files.

She began trying to confide in me several days later.

"I'm still so scared. I don't know where . . . I don't know how to start my story."

"How about with a prayer?"

She closed her eyes and sobbed silently while I asked the Lord to help her, to help me, to provide for Safe House.

"Does this religious bit really work?"

"You'll see. The Lord helps me when I need it. And I know I'm going to heaven because I believe He died for my sins."

"You're a crazy kind of cop."

I laughed. "I've heard that before." Then I spoke as reverently as I knew how. "But you'll see, and I'm going to keep on praying that you'll believe."

She said she wanted to and, straightening her shoulders, told me how she'd nearly been to hell already.

Ginger's gaming took a long time. She began dating Barry, the man who ultimately became her pimp, when she was in the ninth grade. They became lovers. A year later she

63

quit school, left her home, and moved in with him. She wanted a real family.

"With love and security. I wanted to be important to someone."

All this time, Barry, who was older and knew his way around, had a string of girls working for him. He was gone a lot, but Ginger thought that was part of his job. She didn't find out about the girls until much later when Barry said he needed her help. Times were tough, he lamented. She'd have to go to work.

"My baby was almost a year old and I was bored sitting around the house. I told him sure, I'd go to work. But I didn't think a high school dropout could earn much."

Ginger remembered Barry's confident wink and assurance that she'd "be surprised." She shuddered when she recalled the first time he brought a stranger home with him, got her hopelessly high on drug-laden drinks, and put her to bed with the man.

"After that, it never stopped."

If she complained, Barry protested that she didn't love him enough to do her part. Later, he flew into rages and began beating her. From there on it was a familiar story. Fear, pain and ever-increasing doses of drugs became the biggest part of her life. She neglected her baby and finally lost him to the social workers.

"I bottomed out. Then I heard about Lynn coming to this place. And I thought . . ." She began to shake. "Anything would be better. Hey, I need something."

Withdrawal symptoms. I'd seen them so many times before. Thank God I knew what to do. Midwest Challenge was set up to help.

As her health improved, Ginger's mind cleared. She seemed to trust me more and more. She said she'd met Candy on the street and might be able to help me find her.

"If she's still around."

"What do you mean?"

"She maybe got taken to New York. Sometimes that's where they take the problem children."

The pipeline again. Working with Ginger and Lynn, keeping up with my police assignments, and supervising Midwest Challenge hadn't left much time to search for solutions to the other problems I'd pledged to solve.

Ginger saw my expression change. Reading anger on my face, she recoiled.

"What did I do?"

"Nothing." Very gently, I explained everything I wanted to accomplish. "I need all the help you can give me."

Tears began running from her eyes. "You sound like him."

"Who?" My shoulders slumped. I guess I

already knew she thought I was gaming her.

"Barry."

"Look, you don't have to worry about . . ."

"It's not that. Only when you reminded me of him," she lowered her eyelids, "I realized I still love him."

I shook my head. Sometimes a hooker's love for her pimp, regardless of how cruel his treatment, was a hard habit to break.

"Ginger, that doesn't make sense. Think about it."

"I have." She was breathless, sounding desperate.

Fearing I'd ruin my advice with profanity, I took a deep breath. "A pimp's love, or whatever you call it, is no good. It's a destructive thing. Look, when you love the Lord He can give you a new life. The kind of life you said you wanted for your son."

"Okay, okay." The edge on her voice was hardening. "Can I go to my room now?"

It was difficult to let her go. I was anxious to learn more about the Minnesota connection with New York. But I nodded. "We'll talk some more tomorrow."

It didn't work out that way. Ginger sneaked away from Safe House during the night.

Chapter 7

Fighting the power of the pimps was not easy.

Lynn said she'd expected Ginger to return to Barry. When I asked why she hadn't warned me, she shrugged. Sometimes it seemed none of the girls from the street could ever learn to really trust a man again.

I seldom got discouraged. When I did, my wife reminded me of what I so often told others.

"God will help you work it out."

What a wonderful helpmate, I thought, with such a strong faith. It's a pretty foreign concept for the average wife to imagine her husband working so closely with other women, let alone prostitutes. My wife accepted it, understood and was trying to help me keep my commitments.

Still searching for solutions to the problems connected with prostitution, I sat down at my desk and reviewed what I'd learned, wondering if I'd paid enough attention to the psychological elements involved.

Society had fostered many erroneous ideas about prostitution. Women rarely made whores of themselves. Mostly men created prostitutes. It was important for parents, especially fathers, to understand how instrumental they could be in pushing their daughters toward a life walking the streets or working the brothels disguised as health clubs and rap parlors.

The first step to prostitution was usually taken at home. Most young hookers came from fatherless homes or had fathers that were weak. Weakness did not refer to physical strength but to an emotional void. Many men had hang-ups about the outward show of emotion toward their families. The macho image left little room for children to feel the secure warmth of a father's arms, to hear the reassuring words "I love you." When girls didn't sense such love they tended to develop a low opinion of themselves. They felt inadequate.

Prostitutes told me many times, "We make lousy lovers." Sure, maybe they knew every trick of their trade, but usually such expertise was used to generate a *quick* thrill. Time was money. Why even pretend love when lack of it was what usually drove them into strange beds in the first place.

I looked out onto the dark street that ran by my home. Beyond the light cast by the lamp in the window, it was a lonely place. I thought about my children, sound asleep. Were their dreams happy? I thought so. But just in case, I tiptoed into the bedroom and hugged them both while whispering, "I love you."

My wife, Gayle, smiled when I returned to the living room. "You'll find a way."

I hoped so. Even as we sat safely in our comfortable home, thousands of girls were suffering all across the country.

"You know," I said, "I wonder what Xaviera Hollender would have written about prostitution in New York if she'd been run through the Minnesota pipeline."

"There can't be many happy hookers," Gayle agreed.

"You're so right." I'd seen a lot of prostitutes during my career as a policeman and I couldn't remember any that really smiled. A lot of life had been washed out of their faces. Any beauty left was hidden beneath a crust of street makeup.

The next morning, when I visited Safe

House, I saw Lynn beginning to discover her real beauty. The transformation was amazing. Looking at herself in the hallway mirror, she was smiling from ear to ear. The tired, tortured girl that I'd first met in a darkened bar was turning into a gorgeous young lady surrounded by an aura of self-confidence.

She turned to look me straight in the eyes. "I'm sorry I didn't help more with Ginger. I'm sorry I doubted what you were trying to do. But not any more. I know. I believe. I think I've found the Lord."

I didn't speak, just stared, as I felt my face light up like hers.

"What was that Bible verse you told me to read?"

"John 3:3, 'Jesus answered and said unto him, Verily, verily, I say unto thee, Except a man be born again, he cannot see the kingdom of God.'"

"Doesn't that mean women too?"

"You better believe it."

We went back to work, much surer of success.

Lynn gave me more details on the gaming process. The drug most commonly used on new girls was marijuana laced with cocaine, supposedly a sex stimulant. Regardless, when girls got high on the stuff they were easily induced to try whatever was suggested. Most had some previous sexual experience and were eager to impress their new peer group. If not, they were forced.

I already knew how deviate sex acts were used to break down any remaining resistance. Until the girls were void of morals and all they held dear to themselves was destroyed, they didn't make good prostitutes. If degradation didn't work, torture and harder drugs followed. Some uncooperative girls were tied to chairs and had heroin injected into their bloodstreams.

"I've heard of some dying from an overdose," Lynn said angrily. "That's murder."

She was really getting with it, becoming a crusader like me.

When all will finally disappeared, new girls readily joined a new peer group consisting entirely of pimps and prostitutes. A new lifestyle was dictated and at this point the final stage of the gaming process began. Again in a drug-induced state of euphoria, the initiates were encouraged to have sex with different men in the group. They gave them money when they were finished. Caught completely off guard, most girls questioned the payment. The standard answer: "You're a hoe, aren't you?"

"And so," said Lynn, "the gaming ends and the job begins. By that time, anyone surviving really believes she's a whore. And when the partying is over, they come down from their high and find out it's time to go out and work it off."

The entire process, amazing as it seemed, did not take weeks but was often accomplished in twenty-four hours.

"Because of the dope," I thought aloud.

"And fear. Like you already know, the players have refined the art of torture to a degree that will guarantee cooperation."

I jerked my head up from taking notes. "You said that like you were reading from a textbook."

She tried to smile. "I memorized part from an article I read about brainwashing, what they did to American soldiers in the war." Then she started to sob. "But none of us were like soldiers. Just dumb hookers."

I waited until she blinked away the tears. "Good girl. See, it's easier to talk about your past when you know you're forgiven. Now, tell me, where does all this dope you mentioned come from?"

"Some of the pimps are dealers too. They use their hoes like mules." She meant they smuggled drugs.

That was as I expected. Nearly as many young girls were arrested for drug possession as for vice. Few ever talked. They were just as afraid to break the narcotics chain as they were to testify against their pimps. My experiences with Teen Challenge and its drug-education ministry convinced me that the pipeline between Minneapolis and New York's Minnesota Strip ran in both directions—carrying young bodies one way, drugs the other.

"Was organized crime, the Mafia, involved?"

"Maybe. The pimps paid protection sometimes, but I never heard of them owning any girls on the street. Not in Minneapolis anyway." Lynn stopped to rub the furrows appearing on her forehead. "I remember hearing they were into saunas and I suppose they were in on it when some of the classier girls got sent to turn tricks with politicians."

Political whores? I hadn't thought to ask about that, just as I'd forgotten to pursue Lynn's previous reference to corporate prostitution.

"Did they send you?"

She cocked her head. I leaned forward, encouraging a response.

"To politicians?"

I nodded, watching for any sign she'd be afraid to answer.

Lynn sensed my anxiety. "Take it easy. I'm going to tell you everything. I was scared before, when I was running from God. I'm not running any more."

"No, you're not. I'm sorry I doubted you. You're getting to be quite a Christian."

She knew I was referring to her new-found courage. Sitting taller in her chair, she continued. "Yes, my name was passed around among some real bigshots, even a U.S. Senator. I had a reputation for being trustworthy and real good at my job."

But she couldn't nail down any real connections to organized crime. All she remembered was shadow figures that reminded her of movie characters.

"Then tell me more about corporate prostitution."

"That's the way I got started. I worked at it for a couple of years until my pimp gave me to another guy that thought I'd make just as much money and be easier to handle on the street."

"If you were so good, why did your first pimp give you away?"

Lynn started to swear, caught herself, and said, "I guess he got paid something by the other guy. Probably not much. He was mad. He wanted me out."

I still didn't understand.

"Because I had a boyfriend on the side," she continued, beginning to enjoy the story. "My pimp was afraid to beat me when he found out. My boyfriend was a first-string player for the Vikings. He was a sort of pimp too, for other jocks, and he was tough." She whispered his name.

"I always figured he was a pretty clean-cut football player." I began to wonder if everybody making headlines was involved with prostitution.

"He didn't like the all-American jock image. He was into coke too. But he was fun to be seen with. In those days I'd do anything to be noticed, anything for status." She screwed up her face. "Some status. Still, I had it a lot better than most."

As Lynn was beginning to ramble and, forgetting her new status, starting to give lurid descriptions, I interrupted with specific questions.

"Who paid when you helped your pimp, the first one, set up business deals?"

"The company."

"What company?"

She whispered the name of a corporation high on *Fortune* magazine's list of the nation's 500 largest businesses.

"How were you paid?"

"They gave cash to my pimp, I guess. Remember, he worked there."

The pimp handled most of the details and Lynn admitted her memory was mushy.

"I did drugs then, you know."

So there wasn't much more she could tell me.

"But my diary can."

I jumped from my chair, fighting an urge to hug Lynn. Her conversion had been wondrous. Now the treasury of information she promised sounded miraculous.

Chapter 8

Lynn's diary contained names, places, dates, prices, and detailed descriptions of the sexual fantasies of her customers. But it was hidden. She wouldn't tell me where. Even with police protection, she insisted it was too dangerous to retrieve the book immediately.

"I'm not so worried about myself. There's other lives at stake. You'll have to wait. After I've been out of circulation for a while, I'll be forgotten. Then there'll be no problem getting it."

I understood, but I was disappointed nonetheless. It showed in the way the muscles tightened across my jaw.

"Don't pout," she said.

That made me laugh. Here was a young ex-hooker, barely beginning her rehabilitation, assuming a maternal attitude toward a vice cop.

"Besides," she said seriously, "there's plenty of other work to be done. Getting girls off the street and plugging the pipeline to New York seems more important than busting a bunch of bigshots. They'll buy their way out anyway."

I wasn't so sure. The city fathers wanted Minneapolis cleaned up, spotless if possible. But she was right.

"First things first then." I asked if she could put me in touch with anyone who'd been to New York and back.

"Through the pipeline?"

I nodded slowly, not expecting much help.

"Sure. And don't start pouting again." She grinned. "You won't have to wait this time."

Just before she moved into Safe House, Lynn had met an ex-prostitute who encouraged her to get off the streets. The girl had led the same rotten life as Lynn, Ginger and Candy, but now was a Christian.

"She's excited about what you're trying to do at Safe House. I was going to ask her out as soon as I got settled."

"You're settled. And you're a Christian too. You two should have a lot to talk about." I rushed Lynn to a phone.

Happily, the ex-prostitute accepted our invitation to visit Safe House the next day.

Her name was Elaine. She was twenty-one with a look of serene maturity in her deep blue eyes. I would never have guessed she'd worked the streets. Her story started much the same as the others. She was gamed early in high school and worked in Minneapolis until she was eighteen. Then she was taken to New York.

I asked for details.

"Let me start toward the beginning, before my trip to New York. There's some other, very important parts to my story."

I wondered why she smiled.

"Because the Lord really helped me—and someone else. You'll see." She clasped her hands in her lap. "About three years ago, I had a miscarriage. I was in the hospital overnight. When I got out my pimp was waiting to tell me it was time to go back to work. Even though I was sore and felt feverish, I knew I'd better not hassle him. So when he drove to my regular corner, Fifth and Hennepin, I got out of the car and began looking for a john I knew. I had several steady customers who never hurt me and I wanted an easy night."

Lynn began to fidgit. It bothered her to be constantly reminded of past horrors. Both girls agreed it would be easier if Elaine and I talked privately.

"God bless you," said Lynn on the way out.

"And you too."

I could hear in their gentle voices how much each girl meant what she said.

"I used to think that if you trusted in God and things turned bad, then God was a fake. I know better now." Elaine settled into her chair and continued the story.

When there was no action on the corner, she began walking south on Hennepin. Soon she saw Hank coming toward her. Hank was a dentist who'd had regular sex with her for about two years. He once told her that he'd never married because he didn't want to get tied down with a wife and a house full of kids. So he looked for Elaine about twice a week. He was gentle and every time they were finished he gave her a big tip.

But that night she tried to avoid him.

Several weeks before, the last time they were together, Elaine had decided to find out if Hank was as rich as he seemed. She'd encouraged him to drink until he passed out, then searched his apartment. Taped to the underside of an end table, she'd found $2700 in cash and a book showing $106,000 in the bank. Elaine had paced the apartment for hours wondering if she should try stealing the cash or if there was some way to con Hank out of his bank balance. Finally, as he began to awaken, she'd taken several bills and taped the rest back in place. Because Elaine had stayed with him most of the night, Hank gave her double the normal fee. Her pimp had been delighted with the wad of money Elaine brought home, though she hadn't told him where it all came from.

Now Hank was rushing to meet her, smiling. Maybe he hadn't discovered his loss.

"He said he wanted to buy some of my time. When I agreed, he suggested taking me to dinner. I was puzzled. Johns don't take street whores to dinner."

Hank insisted he only wanted to talk that night and thrust five $100 bills into her hand.

"I wondered if he'd gone crazy, but he told me to enjoy the money, 'You know I have plenty.' His wide eyes were staring at me. I figured it was better not to answer."

As they walked to a restaurant Hank told her he knew she'd found his hidden cash and taken some. Instinctively, she started to run but he grabbed her arm and told her everything was okay. He had plenty more. During dinner he pulled out two other bank books. His accounts totalled more than $300,000. Elaine didn't understand why he was showing her so much wealth.

"Wising off, I asked him if he wanted me

to raise my prices. He shrugged his shoulders and said, 'It doesn't matter any more.' Then he began talking about himself."

Hank was a very successful, but miserably lonely, dentist, usually looking like he was about to cry.

"Sitting across from him, playing with my silverware, I wondered what the other people in the restaurant would think if they knew I was a hooker and my john was about to start bawling his eyes out. Then I got quite a shock."

Blinking his eyes he composed himself, Hank leaned across the table and asked Elaine to marry him.

"Other girls on the street talked about johns falling in love with them, but that was the first time for me. I told him to pack sand. I had enough problems living with a pimp who hugged me one minute, reached for his coat hanger the next."

Dry-eyed, Hank wasn't bad to look at— about six feet with a good build, nice hair, an aura of money. But supposing the only one she could love, dared to love, was her pimp, Elaine treated the whole thing as a sick joke.

"I just stared at him, my chest jumping as I laughed silently. He started making a whole bunch of promises. He had enough money to make sure my pimp never found me. I could have a new life, respect, unbelievable happiness . . . I finally told him, 'You're kidding yourself.' "

Changing his approach, Hank began describing a series of messages he'd seen all over town—on billboards, television, and in the newspapers. They were all the same. I FOUND IT, with a telephone number listed beneath. One lonely night, he called the number and was surprised to learn IT meant a life with Christ. The next three nights he watched Billy Graham on television and saw people stepping forward to accept Christ into their lives. Realizing that he was a sinner and that his sins had sent Jesus to the cross, Hank finally got down on his knees and prayed. He confessed his sins and Jesus came into his life.

"I couldn't believe I was earning $500 for listening to a Jesus freak." Elaine looked toward me, swallowing hard, and apologized. "That's what I was thinking then. I shouldn't put it that way now, Mr. Palmquist."

"Why not?" I chuckled. "Jesus freak sounds like a proud title."

She sat straighter in her chair and continued the story.

Hank proposed again, saying he wanted to share his new faith, his love and his money with her.

"For a moment, he looked so happy and

content. Like he expected me to say 'yes.' I almost did, but then I remembered what my pimp always said, 'A hoe, same as a leopard, ain't never gonna change her spots.' So I turned tough and told Hank I didn't want any part of him or his damn religion."

And she got up to return to the street. On the way out, looking over her shoulder, Elaine saw Hank with his head on the table, sobbing. When she suddenly realized he was crying for her, she started to run from the scene, from "the crazy idea that the stupid jerk really loved me. From IT."

The $500 in her purse was enough to convince her pimp that she'd been a very busy girl. With time to spare but no plans for what to do with it, she checked into a hotel, ran a hot tub and turned out all the lights. Her mind became a battleground, the words I FOUND IT flashing like exploding bombs. She soaked for hours trying to clear her head. Memories assaulted her. She might have found IT long ago. As a little girl, her parents had driven her to a church for Sunday school but they'd never followed her inside. At home, they'd fought constantly. When she was about thirteen, Elaine's mother had told her, "Never trust a man," men are no good. If Elaine wanted to get anywhere in life, she'd have to learn to use men. Sex was the perfect way. Her mother'd said. "No man can turn down a good piece of . . ." She'd patted Elaine's fanny. Money had always been a problem. Though her father had earned good wages, he drank too much and gambled them away.

Elaine stopped talking to look at me. She squinted, as if trying to make a judgment.

"I wish my father'd been like you and other Christian men. But he was spineless." She closed her eyes and took a deep breath as she transported herself back to the time in the bathtub.

The fact she'd been confirmed in her church made little difference. It was an empty memory. As other kids had rushed to the rear of the church to receive hugs, kisses and congratulations from their families, Elaine had slipped out a side door to meet her parents in the parking lot. They'd pointed to a package on the back seat of the car and muttered, "Your confirmation gift." Then her father had driven quickly away. No hug, no kisses. Nothing at all.

After that, her morality had begun to disintegrate. It hurt to remember what started happening to her.

"I was beginning to look like a prune anyway. So I jumped out of the tub and into bed. Hoping to sleep. I couldn't. Usually, I didn't have many feelings. The years on the street sort of drained my nerve endings. But that night I was tingling with sensations I didn't understand. And I couldn't make myself forget those words, I FOUND IT. When I finally did drift off to sleep, I dreamed about finding IT. But the next day I was back on the street waiting to be motioned over by a john."

Elaine was beginning to shiver with emotion. Her voice was hoarse. Though I was anxious to hear the end of the story and begin probing for information about the Minnesota pipeline, I knew it was time to stop for the day. I stood up and stretched.

"I'm getting sore from sitting."

"Thanks for being so understanding," she said.

I nodded, beginning to smile. "I think I have a great idea. How about having lunch with a whole gang of Jesus freaks tomorrow?"

Chapter 9

Lunch at Midwest Challenge was scheduled for noon the next day. By one o'clock the soup, still on the stove, was bubbling down to a thick stew and the salads were beginning to wilt.

"I should never have let Elaine go until she finished her story and told me about New York," I fretted. Then, seeing my wife Gayle's disapproving glance, I corrected myself. "Sorry, that's secondary. What I'm really worried about is her safety. I should have sent someone to drive her out here. If the pimps discovered she was coming to talk to me, they may have abducted her."

Or worse, I could see Gayle was thinking. I started to dial police headquarters. Maybe my fellow officers could find Elaine in time.

The front door slammed. Lynn rushed into the room.

"It's okay. Elaine's down the block at Safe House. I was showing her my room and we got to talking and . . ." She stopped to catch her breath.

"And like all children, you forgot the time." I snorted.

Lynn bit her lip.

Gayle stepped forward. "Now, I suppose Elaine's too embarrassed to show up." Smiling, she took Lynn by the arm and went to fetch our guest.

After the meal, which somehow didn't taste as bad as it looked, Elaine followed me to my office and went on with her story.

It had taken over two months for her to begin to get Hank and his I FOUND IT out of her mind. During that time she buried herself deeper and deeper in the garbage dump of prostitution. She started selling herself for group sex, exhibitions with lesbians, and to sado-masochists. She used drugs heavily.

"Before I could do a trick I'd need some reds to help me forget what was going on."

Winter came. She walked the streets in below zero weather, hustling business when other girls hung close to the bars to avoid frostbite. Just before Christmas her pimp said she was doing so well that she deserved a better territory—New York City.

"He promised big money, more money than I'd ever dreamed of, and a glamorous life. 'Baby, you can walk in furs and pull down five or six hundred a night,' he said. 'You're going to be really important.' He wanted me to help keep an eye on three 'chili-dog hookers' that were going along."

He bragged that the other girls would earn big money too. They were young enough to be tight and all were blond, blue-eyed Scandinavian types. Elaine was jealous. She pouted. Her pimp punched her in the mouth and went for his whip.

"'Ungrateful bitch,' he said. He showed me what happened to hoes that didn't appreciate what their men were doing for them." She shuddered. "I can still feel the fiery pain. It was the worst whipping I'd ever had, even though he was careful not to make permanent scars on my body. He hit slowly, working up the backs of my legs and low on my back. When the blood began to ooze from the welts, he knocked me to the floor and tied my ankles to table legs."

I wanted to make her stop, skip the part about how he beat the soles of her feet.

"No, Mr. Palmquist, you need to know. Maybe then you'll be a little more determined to help other girls."

89

The pain was unimaginable. Never strong enough to offer release in unconsciousness, it was like so many long needles thrust upward through her body until even her head felt bloody. The room looked red.

"He stopped for a little while. Long enough to bring the baby whores in to watch. Then he kept slashing at my feet until they held their ears, begging him to stop my screaming."

Finally, the pimp asked if she'd learned her lesson. She whimpered, "Yes." He made her shout the answer, then asked if she still loved him and made her scream "yes" again. Afterward, still in front of the others, he had sex with her.

The next day the four girls were loaded into a late model, customized Cadillac with a television set in the back seat.

"And, would you believe it, those dumb teenie boppers watched cartoons all the way east."

Arriving in New York City late at night, the pimp took his stable of whores to a west side apartment. There they met Rodney, a huge brute who was to be their new handler. All the girls were told to strip. Rodney seemed pleased that the younger girls were all "real blonds." He frowned when he saw Elaine had had a recent lesson. Studying her swollen feet, he wondered if she could walk the long route along the Minnesota Strip.

"My pimp said, 'sure,' then glowered when he saw the unhappy look on my face. I never figured I'd have to work the streets in New York. I thought Big Apple hookers went on call to fancy hotels and apartments in those super tall buildings." Elaine sighed as if to tell me how stupid she'd been.

Rodney began their education immediately. He showed them a map with red lines marking the Minnesota Strip, Eighth Avenue from 42nd Street to 51st Street. Winking at the 'chili-dog hookers,' he explained that was where "all the johns looking for blonds go to score." During the lecture, Rodney outlined the prices to be charged and explained how to avoid trouble with the New York cops. They didn't really care what whores did as long as no public disturbances or felonies occurred. Usually, if busted, a whore was only fined. No more than she could work off in one night, he observed. As a matter of fact he knew of one girl who'd been busted for prostitution eighty-two times and never spent a night in jail. New York City was alike a granddaddy pimp, assessing and collecting fines, giving girls another reason to sell themselves.

Pimps liked to operate in New York City because girls sixteen and over were not considered juveniles. There was little worry about charges of contributing to the delinquency of a minor, child abuse and similar crimes.

"After all," Elaine told me sadly, "it's pretty hard to tell a fourteen-year-old hooker from a sixteen-year-old. And while I was there not many cops seemed to look closely, let alone ask."

A hooker's work day was much longer in New York City. At nine o'clock the next morning Rodney and the Minneapolis pimp drove the girls to Times Square. Turning south on Eighth Avenue they cruised to Thirty-First Street. Elaine couldn't believe how many whores were out so early. Sex shops, nude dancing shows, massage parlors and porno palaces were all open. She wondered if she could make enough money with so much competition.

"I asked Rodney if there were enough customers to go around. He told me not to worry and winked at my pimp. That's when I got worried. I was still thinking of him as 'my pimp,' 'my man,' and he wasn't anymore. I'd been sold or traded or . . ." Elaine crossed her arms over her breasts. "It was bondage, Mr. Palmquist. Bondage."

She also worried about being too old, not tight like the baby whores. Rodney reassured her. She was getting an audition later in the day and, if she tried real hard, he knew she'd pass. Then he let the other girls out of the car and told them to start walking back toward Times Square, warning that they'd better have $200 apiece by the time they got there.

Rodney took Elaine back to the apartment and told her to get ready for a try-out. She was really scared, not knowing who or what to expect. From the bedroom, as she was applying fresh makeup with trembling hands, she overheard Rodney closing his deal with her former pimp. Rodney would send half of the girls' first month's earnings to Minneapolis or, as an option, return some worn down girls with a "little shipment of special stuff." She figured the "special stuff" was dope, probably heroin or cocaine.

"Lots of it comes in through New York, you know."

I knew, just as most law enforcement people knew marijuana and hash was shipped into Texas, Florida and southern California. I wondered what prostitution pipelines ran in those directions. But whoa, I thought, one thing at a time.

Rodney auditioned Elaine himself. In one long session he made her use every trick she knew.

"He was into every part of my body and made me use . . ."

93

I held the palm of my hand in front of her face. "No need to be explicit. I've heard it all before."

She nodded appreciatively. "And you're one of the few men I've met that doesn't get off on porn talk. That's why I trust you."

Exhausted and without a meal all day, Elaine was forced to work her first shift on the Minnesota Strip that evening. Her quota was the same as the others, $200. After walking several blocks without a pick-up she wondered if it was worth going on. The building she leaned against was dirty grey. The sidewalk was littered with paper, some of it pages torn from pornographic magazines. Garbage cans were tipped over between parked cars. People were moving everywhere. Most were hookers and johns. The other, fresher girls, were making lots of pickups. Elaine knew that if she didn't get going there'd be another lesson in store for her.

Half way to Times Square, a little fat guy about forty years old motioned her to stop. He asked if she was a "working girl," another not so subtle street expression for hooking. When she made herself smile he inquired about the price for "two hours of crazy stuff." She was relieved when he agreed to fifty bucks an hour. Maybe she could make him like her well enough to earn her quota.

He took her to his hotel room around the corner and made her show her versatility for over an hour. Finally, as he lay limp on the bed, she had time to rest and go to the bathroom where she popped a couple of reds.

"I was using at least a dozen a day by then. Do you know why?" She answered before I could speak. "Believe it or not, Mr. Palmquist, I was still trying to forget I FOUND IT."

The fat john called for her again and, as she was crossing the room, she was shocked to see a case of Bibles in the corner. When asked, he admitted he sold them, then told her to "shut up" and earn her money. Seeing the Bibles reminded her of Hank. She backed away from the bed.

"I shouted at that sick, two-faced slob, 'What's a Bible salesman doing messing around like this?' He threw me out without paying me. I was too tired and depressed to work any more that night, even if it meant a beating. So I called Rodney and asked him to come for me."

The pimp had his own sense of justice and a crazy sense of humor. When he heard Elaine's story, he kicked the john's door down and beat him instead of her. He took all the man's money and left him lying on the floor under a pile of Bibles.

"Rodney knew the man wouldn't call the

police. Johns seldom do. They've got too much to hide."

After that first night, Rodney wasn't so easy. He demanded that Elaine earn more and more. Finally, the only way she could get enough money to satisfy him was to rip off the johns. She spiked their drinks and rifled their pockets when they passed out. Her best haul was from an executive type at the Holiday Inn on 57th Street. She got a watch, ring, credit cards and $716. She gave Rodney everything except the pack of credit cards and $200 which she saved in case she ever had a slow night or needed to sneak away to rest. Later, when the pimp found the credit cards in her purse, he stripped her piece by piece looking for more loot. He found the $200 in her shoe and went wild, beating her for nearly an hour. Then he sent her to bed with a warning "You better never hold out on me again and you better be ready for work in the morning."

Elaine tensed, then squirmed in her chair. She was reliving every moment of pain. But I hesitated to interrupt. The story's ending seemed too important to her.

Just before dawn one of the baby whores came in with salve for Elaine's cuts. The girl told her that the pimp from Minneapolis was returning with a new group of hookers. Elaine had better make a lot of money dur-

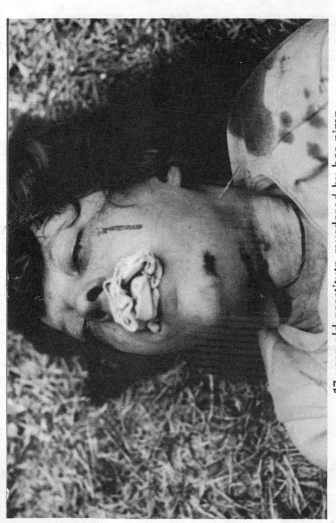

17-year-old prostitute murdered by her pimp

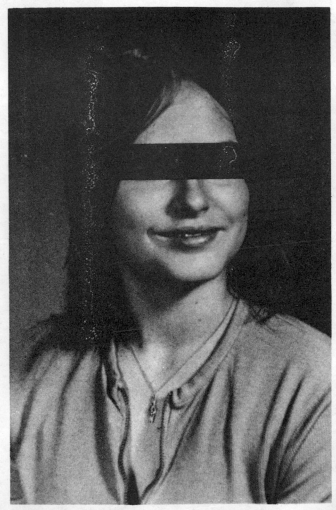

Becky's junior high school picture

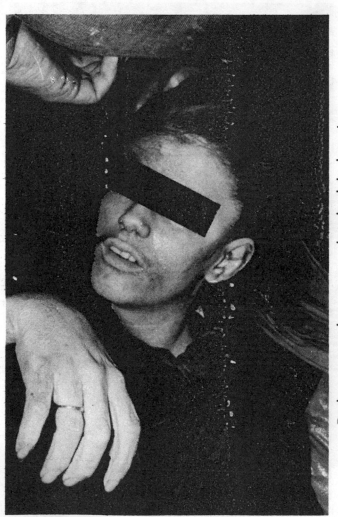

Becky one year later, tortured to death by her pimp

Teenage prostitutes solicit motorists in Minneapolis
Photo Credit: Laurie Jean Schendel

The authors and ex-prostitutes explain the Minnesota Connection to the press.

Photo Credit: Laurie Jean Schendel

Al Palmquist counseling an ex-prostitute

Photo Credit: Hugh Patrick Brown, People Weekly

Questioning Minneapolis prostitutes

Photo Credit: Hugh Patrick Brown, *People Weekly*

Sex show on the Minnesota Strip
Photo Credit: Laurie Jean Schendel

Conducting business on the Minnesota Strip

Photo Credit: Laurie Jean Schendel

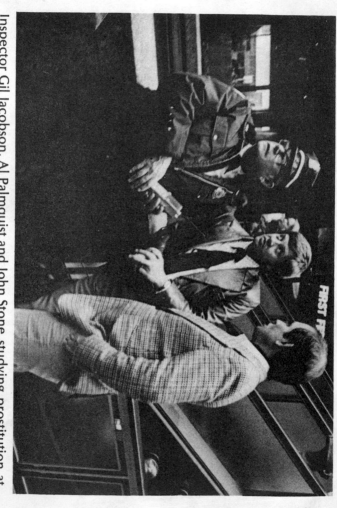

Inspector Gil Jacobson, Al Palmquist and John Stone studying prostitution at Crystal Court

Photo Credit: Laurie Jean Schendel

Minneapolis Police Chief Elmer Nordlund discusses
The Minnesota Connection with the authors
Photo Credit: Laurie Jean Schendel

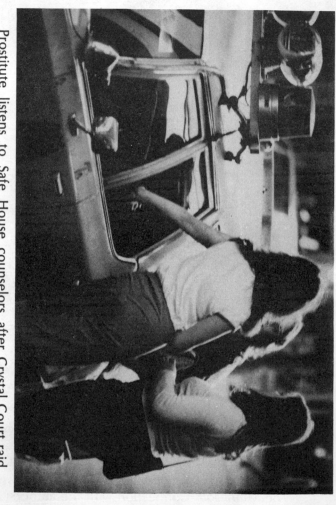

Prostitute listens to Safe House counselors after Crystal Court raid.
Photo Credit: Laurie Jean Schendel

John Stone interviews Minneapolis Mayor Albert
Hofstede
Photo Credit: Laurie Jean Schendel

One of eleven Midwest Challenge residences

Photo Credit: Laurie Jean Schendel

A moment of relaxation for the Palmquist family

Photo Credit: Hugh Patrick Brown, *People Weekly*

Al Palmquist taking a call on the "Hotline to Freedom."

Photo Credit: Laurie Jean Schendel

ing the next few days. Otherwise, she could become excess baggage and get sent back to Minnesota or "just sent away. Know what I mean." The younger girl looked genuinely concerned. Elaine was frantic. What if she couldn't earn or steal enough? The street aged a girl quickly. She was beginning to look too old. Her former pimp must have stopped loving her before he sold her. Now he wouldn't want to be bothered with a failure, someone who'd embarrass him when other pimps were bragging about their younger, prettier hoes. She knew too much to be turned loose. So she'd probably be "just sent away"—killed.

"I knew I had to run, but I didn't know where. I struggled to open a window. It seemed to take forever. I was still weak from the beating and the window had been painted shut. Finally, I climbed out onto a ledge that was about four feet from the fire escape. I jumped, not caring if I missed and fell. The fire escape swayed when I landed. A broken part banged against the building. I stumbled down the rest of the way to the street and began running, afraid Rodney had heard the noise and was already after me. Soon I was lost in the huge city where the only place I really knew was the Minnesota Strip. I was broke, barefoot and wearing just a pajama top under my coat. Then I remembered

Hank and his I FOUND IT. I started to cry. I wanted to call him and ask him for help even if I had to live his way. But I didn't have a dime." She blotted her eyes with a shredded kleenex held in trembling hands.

The story was getting to me too and, when I couldn't find any change in my pockets, I lowered my head. "Our Father, who art in heaven..."

Chapter 10

Elaine's composure returned after we prayed together. My determination to plug the prostitution pipeline boiled over.

"I've got to go to New York," I shouted, "and try to end this sordid brutality."

"I think what I'm going to tell you will make it easier," she said.

Without money there seemed no way to escape from New York. Elaine searched for a trick, but the only guys on the streets at dawn were cops. Remembering that Rodney had told her most cops didn't like to make an arrest toward the end of their duty shift (too much time-consuming paperwork and no overtime pay), she decided to try asking one for a dime.

"One last chance to call Hank for help."

The policeman didn't give her the dime. He was going off duty and he took her home with him instead. Though he was young and good looking, with curly hair sticking out from beneath his policeman's hat, she supposed he was no better than the usual trash that took her to bed. So she was surprised when he introduced her to his roommates, three other cops, and announced "we're all Christians."

They were also rookies, on the force for less than four months. At first, Elaine wondered what a few young Jesus cops could do to help any whore in a city with a reputation for police corruption. All she wanted was the use of their phone.

An answering service told her Hank was on vacation for two weeks. She slammed the receiver down and began to swear. Then she heard the policemen praying that God give her inner peace and a calm spirit. And she realized why she'd been trying to call Hank. She trusted him. He'd FOUND IT. And so apparently had the four rookies in the room with her. Not knowing if her tears were all from happiness or part from frustration and fear, she told them what had happened to her. With a strange new modesty, she showed them her bloodied body. One gagged. Another closed his eyes. None had seen the results of a coat hanger whipping before. They wanted to arrest Rodney immediately.

"I refused to bring charges. I was still too scared." Elaine looked at me hopefully.

I understood. But I also explained that the police could never rid the streets of the Rodneys unless girls like her testified against them.

"Now there's a place for girls like you to be safe." I swept my hand in a wide arc indicating Midwest Challenge and Safe House. Then I encouraged her to go on with the story. I wanted to know more about the Christian cops. "Were they the only ones?"

"They said there were others, some rookies like them and quite a few old-timers. But we didn't talk much more that morning. I was exhausted. They put me to bed." She grinned. "*Alone.* As I was dozing off I heard one say sleep was a great healer. Another reminded him that Christ was the greatest healer."

Dreaming about I FOUND IT, Elaine slept for fifteen hours. It was dark and quiet when she awoke. She felt okay but at first she didn't know where she was. Then Elaine heard whispers and the cops tiptoeing around their house. They were getting ready to go on duty. A long note had already been pinned to her pillow. The light was dim. She only read the end. "Rest and let the Lord watch over you, Elaine. There's food in the refrigerator, clothes by your bed, and no need to worry. We'll be home in the morning. Love."

"I still didn't understand all the love business Christians talked about. What kind of love? I'd loved my pimp. I'd made love to more men than I could ever count. Love sounded sort of mean and dirty to me. And I was suddenly as scared as before. Only it was a new kind of fear."

Elaine feigned sleep until the policemen left. She thought she wanted to find IT. But she wasn't really sure IT wanted to be found by her. She was a whore knowing only a life of sex and drugs. The idea of finding Christ, meeting the standards set down in the Bible, was indeed frightening.

Carrying the note with her, she explored the house. A place had been set for her at the dining room table. A new toothbrush waited for her in the bathroom. Everything was almost as if the house expected to be her home. But it was too much for her tortured mind to handle. She hurried back to the bedroom and dressed quickly. And ran again.

The tall buildings were far away on the horizon. The residential neighborhood through which she tried to find her way was so foreign to Elaine that she traveled in circles, passing the policemen's house twice. The second time around, as she stopped to get her bearings, she realized that she was still carrying the note. Catching light from the window, she read from the beginning. "We have to go to work but you'll be safe here. We'll be praying for you. We know you may dread your first meeting with Christ and think about leaving us. But remember, He has taken much worse sinners than yourself into His arms. They've found salvation. So will you." The rest she already knew. And she was beginning to see a new meaning for love. Tears streaming from her eyes, she went back into the house and began practicing to pray.

The rookies brought another, older cop home with them. He was a vice detective who wanted to bust Rodney. Elaine's terrible fear of reprisal returned. When the rookies told her that God had a plan for her, Elaine wondered if they were using God to game her.

"I screamed at them. 'God doesn't make plans for whores. Only pimps make plans for whores.' The older guy sat down beside me and said, 'Listen, girl, I'm not as much of a churchgoer as these four rookies, but I do know that when Jesus Christ was on earth He had a good friend who'd been a hooker.

She found a better way to live and I'll bet she ended up going to heaven. Why not you?" Elaine smiled at me. "And, do you know, that tough old cop never asked me another thing about Rodney."

"Well *I'm* going to."

"For sure. But not until I've finished my story." She grinned at me. "Or have you already guessed the ending."

After the vice cop left, the rookies asked if Elaine was ready to accept Jesus Christ into her life. She still wasn't sure. She wanted to know more about the plan they said God had for her. It was in the Bible, they said. It was the same basic plan for everybody that believed—help others.

"And now do you see how specifically you can apply yourself to that plan?" I interrupted.

Again she grinned. "Are you recruiting me, Mr. Palmquist?"

"You betcha. I may even take you to New York."

Her face glowing, she described her first steps toward Christ. "The Jesus cops asked if I was ready. I said, 'Sure,' but I didn't know how. They promised it was easy and asked me to repeat after them, 'Jesus, thank you for loving me. Jesus, I confess I'm a sinner. Please forgive my sins. Jesus, I open my heart to you now. I give you my life. Thank

you, Jesus, for taking me into your family.'"
Elaine cocked her head, studying my face
before speaking again. "I've never said this
to anyone before but, you know, for a minute after I'd repeated all they asked I thought
it was still another game. Then I felt my
body relax. I actually slid out of my chair
onto the floor where I began to cry. Not
tears of pain like before, but my very first,
really happy tears. I FOUND IT."

I was feeling as warm and comfortable as
Elaine. We just sat and looked at each other.
I guess we were both marveling—a vice cop
and an ex-hooker sharing God.

During Elaine's years on the street, her
mother had died and her father had been
committed to a mental institution. Her sister,
also a new Christian, came east to bring her
home. For the first time in their lives they
could talk together without feeling mistrust.
On the flight to Minneapolis they discussed
their conversions and agreed that though
the first step was a big one taken suddenly,
there was a lot of growing to do afterward.

"I have a good job now. A new identity.
I'm pretty safe." She hesitated, almost looking embarrassed. "But what about the others?
We both know God's plan for me. Ask your
questions, Mr. Palmquist."

The transition from inspirational dialog to
police interrogation wasn't that easy for me.

I fumbled through my notes looking for a place to begin.

"Let me help." She handed me a list of favorite hangouts for pimps in New York. And another of hotels that catered to prostitutes. "I also made a copy of the map Rodney showed me that first day."

"What happened to him?"

"He left town. Moved to the west coast. There's a Minnesota Strip in L.A. too, you know."

I didn't, but as soon as I had time I was going to check into it. Whoa. Again I had to caution myself. First things first. Better to do a good job plugging one pipeline at a time.

"Elaine, how does a Minneapolis pimp make a contact in New York?"

"The connections are usually between transplanted pimps and their old buddies. Most criminals move in and out of the Big Apple as the heat is turned on and off. Then there's the guys running from the law in Minneapolis. They figure they can hide better in a bigger city."

"So the contacts all originate with the criminal element."

"You're the cop. You should know prostitution is interconnected with everything from dope dealing to armed robbery, blackmail. . . ." She threw her hands up in the air.

"Sure I know. Only the happy hookers

described in some books threw me off the track for a minute."

"The classy girls are the ones that dance to the syndicate's tune."

I went on to ask her for details about transportation schedules, pick-up and drop-off points, communications procedures, and pay-offs; all the dirty wheels of the pipeline mechanism. She didn't have many answers. Apparently there was little leadership, each pimp working the system as he saw fit. The only common denominator was the fear factor.

"Without it, there'd be hundreds of girls blabbing their heads off."

That was one of the reasons for Safe House. Once girls began to fill it up, the law enforcement agencies and I would have plenty of answers and lots of convictions.

An hour later, Elaine had told me all she knew about the Minnesota Connection. I had only two questions left.

"What about Hank?"

"He knows I FOUND IT. Now we go to the same church." Her smile broadened. "Soon . . ."

If I had a bell, I'd have rung it.

Some of the joy drained out of me when I asked about Candy. "Ever meet her?"

Elaine's face saddened too. She wasn't sure. "There are a lot of Candys. And Al,

I've been thinking. You're going to feel hurt, you know, because you can't help them all."

I started to nod slowly. Then I stood up. "I can try."

Chapter 11

Safe House was operative, but nearly empty. Leaves falling from the trees outside reminded me that plans to recruit occupants from among the girls selling themselves in the bars and byways of Minneapolis were far behind schedule. Though I'd intended to combine my police work with spiritual therapy for young prostitutes I realized that most of my time was spent researching the problems I faced.

Aware there was still much to learn, I nonetheless decided to begin an active campaign. The Mayor, Police Chief and my superiors in the Division of Community Relations agreed. There was, however, a serious question of cooperation from certain segments of the business community and other law enforcement agencies, especially in New York.

"Forget the Big Apple," suggested the Captain. "Concentrate on the home front."

"The pipeline connects Minneapolis to New York. Unless we plug it, the pimps will only move their business eastward when we clamp down. That won't help save the girls," I insisted.

"You're right," he admitted. "But you're going to have a devil of a time convincing the politicians and the good citizens of New York that prostitution isn't a victimless crime."

"Baloney," I said. But I knew he was right.

Psuedo-enlightened society in most major cities believed the myths that allowed 'victimless' to be used in describing an often heinous crime. Their argument was based on the premise that "consenting adults have a right to behave as they please": law enforcement should not concern itself with morality. The fact they hadn't read the Bible might be their business. But failure to study the myths as they related to documented facts was another matter. Making the assumption that the average prostitute was a happy, healthy-minded adult was not only ridiculous, it was a dangerous distortion. Decriminalizing or legalizing prostitution would add to the destruction of more than morality. It would kill, one way or another, many girls not yet old enough to vote.

"Completely ready or not, I'm going to move in on the Minneapolis pimps and, as soon as possible, I'm going to make big waves on the eastern seaboard." I told my wife when I got home that night.

As usual, Gayle encouraged me.

"You're a wonder," I said. "Doesn't it ever bother you that your husband spends most of his time working with younger women whose lives have been devoted to sex?"

She shook her head. "That's a silly question. Someone has to help those girls. The Bible has a lot to say about helping prostitutes, you know. Though I do worry about your safety sometimes. The people you're fighting are as mean as they come."

Later, as I was preparing for bed, the phone rang. Gayle's face paled when she answered it.

"It's Lynn. There's trouble."

Lynn had located Ginger several weeks before and was keeping in touch with her by phone. There was a strong possibility Ginger would return to Safe House; if not as a resident, certainly as an 'out patient.' Already, Ginger had moved away from her pimp and taken a straight job. Now, her pimp was applying pressure.

"I just talked with Ginger. She sounded really frightened. She said her pimp was there trying to scare her with words. But I think she meant he was about to get violent." Lynn's voice cracked. "When she said 'goodbye' it sounded like she thought she was going to die."

I already knew the address of Ginger's apartment. Dressing with one hand, I dialed the police station in the suburb where Ginger lived and asked for assistance. Then, strapping on my gun, I ran to my car.

Ginger lived about twenty minutes from my home. That night I cut the driving time in half, thankful that my one extravagance was a fast sports car. Skidding to a stop and leaving the car double parked, I rushed into Ginger's building. Red lights flashing in the distance signaled help was on its way. Ginger's door was closed but not locked. I slipped into the apartment with my gun drawn. There was no sound. Nothing moved. A single lamp lying sideways on an end table cast long shadows across the living room. Broken furniture was scattered everywhere. A wild pattern of dark stains criss-crossed the carpet. Blood.

Cautiously, I checked the other rooms. They were torn up also, but empty. Returning to the living room I heard a moan from behind the sofa and saw a hand clawing at the wall for support. Ginger struggled to her feet, then collapsed into my arms. I felt her blood begin to soak through my shirt.

Other policemen rushed into the room. Together we examined Ginger.

"Better call an ambulance," one said.

"No, no. I'll be okay," Ginger protested.

I knew that, like Candy, she hated hospitals. She equated them with jail. But she needed attention. The pimp had beaten her with a wine bottle and smashed a lamp on her head.

"I'll take you myself," I promised. "Now, tell me, where's your pimp?"

She refused to answer. The other cops looked for evidence while I administered first aid. Ginger's scalp was torn in a dozen places. Pressure bandages stopped the bleeding but she'd need stitches and I was afraid of infection.

On the way to a doctor I asked again about her pimp.

"I don't want you to arrest him. He'll just get loose on bail and come after me again. Maybe kill me."

"Look, young lady, if you don't help me get him, he'll hassle you forever. I can't promise what his sentence will be, but I'll guarantee he won't bother you after he meets me. I can be half animal too when I need to be."

While Ginger was being treated I tried to talk her into returning to Safe House. She finally agreed and, accepting my guarantee of protection, took me to the pimp's hideaway.

I crashed in as he cracked the door to peer out. Advising him of his rights, I shoved him against the wall and told him to assume the position. He knew what I meant and spread-eagled himself for a search, staring wild eyed at the 357 revolver I held close between his eyes.

"I should kill you," I growled. "And I may if you ever go near Ginger again."

"I got rights," he whimpered.

"Not to torture people and lead them to hell. Stay away from Safe House." I touched the end of his nose with the gun barrel. "Got it?"

After booking the pimp, I took Ginger home with me. My wife was waiting to help her clean up and get settled for the night.

"Though there isn't much of it left," she said, noticing the first faint light of dawn.

Sleep didn't matter. Ginger's return was sufficient stimulant to keep me going for another twenty-four hours. As soon as the girl was secure at Safe House I planned to comb the city for more like her. And to firm up plans for my first trip to New York.

My initial forays into the vice centers of Minneapolis were disappointing. As the Captain had said, I couldn't detain people for walking and talking together. Without the threat of arrest, few young prostitutes would talk to me. Those that didn't appear frightened were contemptuous of the salvation I promised was theirs for the asking.

"Who needs Jesus? What does He pay? Nothing," spat one.

The girl with her hated cops. "Because I know pigs who sneak up on girls parked with their boyfriends, lock the guy in the squad car, and then go back to tell the girl that if she doesn't come across they'll both get busted. That's how horny pigs root for their kicks."

Another, looking to impress her grinning pimp, told me that any cop packing a Bible and trying to talk people out of having a 'good time' had to be queer.

"A freak," muttered the pimp.

I was angry, but I let them go and returned to Safe House wondering what I was doing wrong.

Lynn and Elaine, who was visiting Safe House regularly, thought maybe I'd been trying to preach too much too soon.

"We know Jesus said that if you know the

truth, the truth will make you free. But most girls on the street have no idea what the truth is. They don't even know what love is," Elaine said. "Remember how long it was before I FOUND IT."

"Try being *loving tough,* the way you were with us. Sell yourself first," added Lynn.

They both laughed. Then Ginger, who'd been listening quietly, stood up, hands on hips, and angrily confronted them.

"This is no time to tease."

"They didn't mean to tease," I told her. "What they say makes a lot of sense. Most girls like you need love more than criticism, understanding more than sermons," I hesitated, remembering Ginger's recent ordeal. "And assurance of safety more than anything."

Ginger nodded, sitting down again.

I rose and began pacing, thinking out loud. "First, I've got to be sure everyone knows about Safe House; that it's a haven where love, Christ's love, can conquer all. That means publicity. Then, I've got to have more help."

"How about us?" Lynn looked toward Elaine.

Ginger jumped up. "And me. I can learn to be a disciple."

Again, the girls had a good idea. Teenagers were always more comfortable communicating with their peers. Neither cops nor clergymen, my girls were nonetheless experienced in the ways of the street and fine examples of the better way of life awaiting others. Even Ginger, fast becoming a believer, was proof that anyone could escape from a life of prostitution if she tried. My girls would need protection, but there were plenty of policemen to provide that.

I ran my ideas by the Captain.

"Might work."

A Sergeant, many years on the vice squad, overheard and observed, "They may listen to your reformed hookers. And since most of the girls come from loveless homes, the love angle just might work."

My eyes widened. The tough old Sergeant sounded like he was endorsing love. "Christ's love?" I asked hopefully.

He shrugged. "Maybe. But look, I'm just a policeman. I'll see the pimps are arrested whenever you and your disciples get the streetwalkers to bring charges. If love, the Bible and a bunch of reformed hookers can do the job, well then . . ."

"Use them," finished the Captain.

Remembering Candy's escape and Ginger's flight from Safe House, I decided the girls should finish phase one of the Midwest Challenge program before beginning work on the street.

In the meantime, I encouraged reporters to run stories about Safe House in the newspapers, and I publicly announced I was leaving for New York to investigate the Minnesota Strip.

Chapter 12

Communication between the Minneapolis and New York police departments had never been good. When the press ran stories about my forthcoming expedition to gather evidence and bring girls home from the Minnesota Strip the attitude of most New York police officials could only be described as hostile. But I'd made contact with Senator Ralph J. Marino, chairman of the New York State Senate's Select Committee on Crime, and been promised whatever help I needed. Hopefully, special liaison between the police departments would be established later.

The morning sky darkened as the airliner approached New York City. The pilot announced the weather ahead was blustery, rainy and forty degrees.

"Not a very good day to find street-walkers," said the vice officer accompanying me.

Two New York City detectives, assigned to work with us, met the plane. They took us to the office of the Select Committee on Crime where a press conference had been arranged. After explaining my mission to a large group of reporters from newspapers, television and magazines, I began to feel like a celebrity. Then, looking out onto the dirty, rain swept streets, I was reminded that Candy and so many others like her were not enjoying such a warm and pleasant atmosphere.

"Can we get to work on the streets?" I asked Jim McKenna who headed the Select Committee's investigation into New York City's prostitution and child pornography.

"The weather and all this publicity may drive most of the girls inside. Certainly it's hurting business . . ." He watched the rain-drops running down the window. "In the long run, however, the rain may improve your chances. In this kind of weather the girls have a hard time making their 'nut.' (Loosely translated, nut was the amount of money a prostitute was expected to earn and bring to her pimp before she could quit for the day.)

"There's probably a lot of pimps in this town really kicking their girls today. Maybe some of the girls will see or read about you and make contact with us. Maybe they'll see this as a good time to get out of the racket," he said.

I started looking for my coat. My associate from Minneapolis suggested waiting. There'd be more activity after dark. Meanwhile, there were pictures to swap. Many parents had given us photographs hoping someone we met in New York City might recognize their runaway daughters. Jim McKenna had his own pictures of prostitutes on the Minnesota Strip. He hoped we'd be able to make match-ups and identifications.

Studying the faces of the girls, some smiling as they posed for school photographers and others scowling as they ducked away from police cameras, I prayed to find Candy. She wasn't among them, nor were any other girls I'd seen before.

"What did you expect?" asked one of the New York City detectives. "There's probably a thousand Minnesota girls selling themselves on our streets. And lots more from other parts of the country. We've been collecting pictures from Detroit, Chicago . . . everywhere in an effort to understand the workings of the national prostitution trade."

The Select Committee on Crime was also holding secret hearings to question prostitutes. Identified only by pseudonyms, they told familiar stories. Some added important details to my mass of research.

Judy Doe, age 15, told how she and a girlfriend got off a bus from Miami and were immediately recruited to become Times Square hookers. They were required to streetwalk for a week, then were transferred to the Star and Garter bar where they danced nude and solicited sexual activities for fees of "$20 on up." She said she worked seven days a week, earning about $150 a day, all of which she turned over to her pimp. He returned $5 a day for her to live on. When the pimp, Huntsberry, decided that "$150 wasn't enough" he transferred the girls to the Broadway Burlesk where they were able to bring in $200 to $250 per ten-hour shift. Customers were serviced in small rooms she described as dimly lit "cubicles" furnished only with a sheet covered foam mattress. A curtain served as a door.

The police officer who eventually arrested Huntsberry told the panel the defendant was able to plea bargain to two misdemeanors for which he was fined $300.

Another witness, Janet Doe, was a 17-year-old runaway from Minneapolis who'd worked three months for a call-girl service that advertised openly in magazines such as *Screw*. Her pimp sent her to the apartment or hotel room of the customer where, for $60 an hour she performed sexual acts including sado-masochism and bondage. The pimp beat her badly when she performed below expectations. She finally ran from him and turned herself in to the police, saying, "I just want to go home."

The pimp was later arrested and sentenced to three years' probation. Recently he'd been seen putting new girls to work.

The many pages of similar testimony indicated that not all girls were transported through the pipeline. They were gamed in New York City the same as in Minneapolis. And they were put to work in a much wider variety of commercial sex than I'd imagined.

Streetwalkers still comprised the majority of prostitutes in New York City and most other places. They were apparently involved only with their pimps. Girls working in topless bars, live peep shows, massage parlors and the call-girl rackets might well be in the clutches of larger criminal organizations.

"But don't assume the pimps aren't organized," said a vice detective. "How do you think they manage such light sentences? They've probably got connections in some very high places. And we think they buy extra protection from the mob."

I took a deep breath. Plugging the Minnesota pipeline was going to be even harder than I thought. Perhaps the war on vice would last beyond my lifetime. Swallowing hard, I straightened my shoulders and stood up. The rain was still falling, but now I needed to see the battlefield for myself.

Followed by a camera crew and a mob of reporters, my associate, the New York detectives and I walked through the stormy night to Times Square.

"This is where the Minnesota Strip begins," said one detective.

The other began describing the greatest nonstop sex carnival in the world, a garish honky-tonk area overrun with hookers, muggers, con artists, pickpockets, panhandlers, pathetic winos and victimized tourists.

Uniformed cops and plainclothesmen were everywhere. They were stationed to stop so-called serious crime; stabbings, stickups and other violence. They generally ignored vice.

"Why?" I asked without enthusiasm. I thought I knew the answer.

"Every police officer could be working twenty-four hours every day and the streets still wouldn't be clean. Besides, it takes eight hours to process an arrest and weeks to prepare a prosecution. Police officers don't get paid overtime and the courts are over-crowded. Law enforcement is a matter of priorities. I guess. Money crimes and violent crimes get the most attention."

I started to ask, "What can be more violent than . . ."

He interrupted. "I know exactly how you feel. I get mad too. But the city government seems to believe there's no way to stop the world's oldest profession. So most of the time they look the other way and crack down just hard enough to make it look like they're try-ing to protect the public morals."

"And the girls are forgotten."

He nodded. There's little attempt made to rehabilitate them. Most never spend any jail time. If they are busted, they plead guilty to a reduced charge, pay a fine and rush back to the street to recoup their money."

"How many arrests last year?"

"Maybe 6000."

"What's the average fine?"

"Between $100 and $300." His lips twisted in a cynical smile. "Yeah, the city gets to share in the profits too."

I held up my hand, signaling him not to take personal offense. "One of my girls once called this city 'the biggest pimp of all.'"

As we walked around Times Square I looked into several porn theaters and peep shows to see if the customers were as raunchy as the environment. There were all types—bluejeaned kids and dressed up tourists, businessmen and blue collar workers, blasé New Yorkers and wide-eyed foreigners, thugs and even cops. Faggots drifted back and forth hoping someone would invite them into a viewing booth. Condom machines were everywhere. The detective explained that was a subtle way of asking customers not to leave evidence of masturbation on the floor in the viewing booths.

I started a list of the sex businesses. Big City Bookcenter sold hard core porn and offered filmed peep shows. A handwritten sign advertised "a few rare copies" of an 8mm movie titled *Pregnant Punishment* featuring a woman in the late stages of pregnancy being tortured by her gynecologist. Adulterama, Pussycat Show Center and the Frisco S & M Theatre offered live peep shows. The Exotic Circus promoted "kinkiness," inferring it had displays of sodomy and other deviate "delights" stopping only at child porn. I wrote down nineteen names before I realized the list could go on forever and stopped in disgust.

One of the detectives began a short history of the area. For over half a century Times Square had been "where it's at" for illicit sex. Once World War I got under way it ran wide open. The general attitude was "boys

will be boys": why deny the brave servicemen a little carnal pleasure? During the post-
war years of Tammany Hall corruption, the
area continued to thrive although there were
the usual election pledges to "clean up Times
Square." Once re-elected the Tammany politicians ignored their promises and continued
amassing wealth from payoffs by the vice
lords. In 1932, when Fiorello H. LaGuardia
became mayor, an honest attempt was made
to stamp out vice. Burlesque, the raunchiest
form of X-rated entertainment at the time,
was closed down along with the "red light
district."

The sex supermarkets reopened during
World War II, when American morals loos-
ened up generally. There was a brief but
sensational outcry against teenage hookers
calling themselves "victory girls." The victory girls were mostly runaways deluding
themselves with the idea of helping servicemen's morale. But public concern was not
for the girls so much as the near epidemic of
VD among servicemen.

After the war new efforts were made to rid
Times Square of vice. In 1948, the City Planning Commission headed by Robert F. Wagner, Jr., denounced conditions allowing the
open sale of sex. By 1954, when Wagner was
elected mayor, police were making periodic
sweeps of the Time Square area, picking up

hookers and closing any business that catered to undesirables. Such activity, however, usually occurred just before elections.

Mayor John V. Lindsey continued the tradition of defending the public morals at the right time. To fulfill an election promise, the Lindsey Cleanup Commandos were sent to purify Times Square. At the insistence of the Broadway Association, a group of businessmen, realtors and owners of legitimate theaters, the city administration embarked on what the New York Times called a "comprehensive effort to drive out the undesirables and discourage commercial ventures that attract them, as part of a general upgrading of the city's entertainment area." But it was only a token crackdown.

By the time Mayor Abraham Beame had been in office four years and was running for re-election the citizens of New York were taking a ho-hum attitude toward vice around Times Square. Beame's obviously politically motivated raids on sex peddlers were ineffective and generally ignored.

"What about the new administration?" I asked hopefully.

The detective shrugged. "Too soon to tell."

We moved on to the Minnesota Strip. Because of the rain most people were standing under theater marquees and in doorways. Many were passing wine bottles, sniffing cocaine or smoking marijuana. One man stood on the corner of 8th Avenue and 43rd Street holding a hypodermic syringe. Two hookers passed us glancing warily over their shoulders. Up ahead they found a man who didn't look like a cop.

I heard one say, "Wanna date, honey?"

The other chorused, "Wanna party? Come on over here, I'll take good care of you."

The man turned them down. "You don't look healthy."

A pimp appeared, gave him the finger, and urged the girls to hurry down the street. "You gotta keep moving. Never stop unless to set a trick. Keep moving and keep looking or you'll never make your nut."

The girls were about seventeen. Beginners. I thought, probably runaways. I wanted to detain them.

"No chance," said one of the detectives. He explained that kids over sixteen were out of juvenile court jurisdictions and that since the year before, when the law was changed, running away from home had not been a crime. "Besides, the girls are nearly impossible to identify. They all use aliases and lie about their age. And proving a solicitation offense is darn near impossible without the testimony of a john. So what can we do?"

The other detective threw his hands out,

palms up. "It's too wet and too late. Tomorrow's another day."

The detectives stayed with us at our motel. The next morning they borrowed our razors and put on the same clothes. They weren't planning on going home as long as we needed them. And they weren't getting paid overtime. Though I thought one was Jewish and the other never mentioned God, they reminded me of the Jesus cops who'd helped Elaine.

"Whether you'll admit it or not, you've got Christian spirits," I told them.

They took us to visit Father Bruce Ritter who knew the scene along 8th Avenue as well as anyone. He ran Covenant, a haven for young prostitutes, male and female.

"Are there many male prostitutes?" I asked him.

"More than you'd imagine and their numbers seem to be growing quickly."

I looked at my associate from Minneapolis. "Will the filth ever stop spreading?"

Father Ritter told us the influx of teenage prostitutes from Minneapolis had also increased considerably. The detectives agreed. They knew of no other comparable inter-city prostitution network.

"How do the Minneapolis pimps make contacts in New York?" I asked, trying to fill the biggest gap in my investigation.

The priest and the detectives told me that my information from Elaine was leading in the wrong direction. Minneapolis pimps didn't bring girls to New York nearly so often as eastern pimps raided the Midwest. New York pimps traveled to Minneapolis with a pitch that girls could make thousands of dollars a week in the Big Apple and that runaways could escape the hassle of the police. Short training sessions, sometimes with the assistance of local pimps, were held in Minneapolis. Then, as soon as the beginners proved themselves and earned enough money for fare they were put on a plane to New York City. Numerous pimps had been identified as plying their trade between Minneapolis and New York.

"But there aren't many girls willing to testify against them, so most are still in business," said one of the detectives.

"That's one of the reasons we're here," I told him. "If we can convince girls to come home to a new life maybe some will find strength and courage enough to help jail some of those well travelled s.o.b.'s."

"That's pretty rough talk, Reverend," said the detective.

"Because I'm angry," I said, clenching my fists. "I know sin never stays the same, but I'm tired of seeing it always get worse."

Chapter 13

Although one goal was to prosecute the pimps, my first priority was to bring girls home. Along with the vice officer from Minneapolis and the two New York detectives, I searched the Minnesota Strip for the next two days. I learned a lot about commercial sex but no one would accept my offer of a free and guaranteed safe trip to a better life.

My associates seemed uneasy with my religious orientation.

"Sometimes I worry that it's just too heavy on these girls heads to go straight from the whore scene into Christianity," said the vice officer.

"It can be done." I told him about Lynn.

"But you can't stamp out sin overnight," he insisted.

"I'm not trying to stamp out sin as much as I'm hoping to give these girls an alternative." I pointed to a tight-skirted teenager soliciting a middle-aged executive type within arms length of the cop on the corner.

The press and film crews followed us everywhere. Noticing the floodlights and popping flash bulbs, the cop on the corner motioned us over.

"Where are you guys from, Hollywood?" I explained our mission.

He frowned. "You're just causing a useless commotion. No way you can stop the action on this street. Look at Father Ritter. He helps a few maybe, but he knows better than to get too pushy. If he really started to cut into this whore thing, they'd just kill him."

"They?"

"The pimps or the mafia. Depends on which girls are harassed. Low class or high class, outsiders or insiders."

I wanted details, but he only shrugged.

Father Ritter was one of the highlights of our trip. He was accomplishing more than most people knew. Actually, Covenant was a kind of safe house, though without police protection. The priest said most patrolmen working the Times Square district began as good guys—some like the rookies Elaine had encountered. They just burned out quickly. Spiritless, they usually chose peaceful co-existence with the vice lords. Corruption was more common in New York than Minnesota-bred prostitutes.

"The worst part of it," he said, "is that the higher up you go, the worse it gets. Police-men on the street try, but they can't begin to stop the vice rackets without support from their superiors. They don't get any. So they give up."

The detectives with us were exceptions. Leaders in the Select Committee's investigation of vice, they encouraged fellow officers to take a long, hard look at the rotten system they were condoning.

"You're not alone, Al. There are plenty of honest New York cops beginning to speak their minds," one of them said. Smile lines formed at the corners of his eyes. "There's even about 200 of those—what did you call them—Jesus cops."

The rain never stopped. As word of my mission spread, girls began disappearing from the Minnesota Strip. We prepared to leave without a single girl in tow.

"Empty-handed. Too much publicity," my traveling companion complained.

"Maybe not. The long-range effect may be quite different."

I was already planning to order printed

cards offering protection, transportation to Minneapolis and a Christ-centered lifestyle. And I was pondering the idea of returning to New York with van loads of Midwest Challenge and Safe House kids—all former drug addicts or ex-hookers, all enthusiastic born-again Christians.

"As you once said, Christians like me are very vocal people," I reminded the vice officer as we settled into our seats on the plane.

It made a lot of sense to use that endowment to broadcast news of the Safe House program.

"The kids who've been to hell and back will make much better recruiters than you and I," I told him.

He thought I was kidding.

"No way."

As quickly as that, while the airliner was breaking through the clouds over New York City, I made up my mind to come back with the best help available. Midwest Challenge could pay for the expedition, just as it had paid for the current trip. With proper supervision and protection its reborn residents would make more of an impression on the streetwalkers than a battalion of policemen.

I wasn't returning empty-handed. The information I'd obtained, my experiences on the street, the contacts with Father Ritter and the leaders of the Select Committee on

Crime were all strategic weapons in battle to break the Minnesota Connection.

My wife didn't waste time telling me not to be discouraged. She knew that if one thing didn't work, I always tried another. The staff at Midwest Challenge and the girls at Safe House applauded my idea to use qualified residents as spokespeople.

"Super," Ginger squealed with excitement. "We'll be true disciples."

Elaine was more reserved, advising me that New York girls might be much harder to work with than their Minneapolis counterparts.

"It's a much tougher life on that Minnesota Strip," she said, closing her eyes sadly.

I reminded her that the girls there needed help regardless of what we both knew and asked her to help me interpret more of the information I'd brought back with me.

Elaine admitted that her experiences might be an exception to the general rule. She'd heard that many New York pimps made forays into the midwest.

"But their movements are top secret," she said. "I think maybe they use the same underground as drug smugglers."

"They've got to be in business together," I agreed. "But proving it's not going to be easy."

"Wait until more girls move in here," she

smiled, then stretched her eyes wide open. A startling, part-serious part-mischievous, expression. "I almost forgot to ask. Rumor has it, you may have a problem with the latest resident. They're keeping her over at the main building."

I didn't know what Elaine meant and she wouldn't tell me, suggesting that I ask the staff instead.

When my co-workers introduced me to the newest resident, my eyes widened too. "She" was a "he"; a young male prostitute who'd been tortured and degraded just like the girls. Without a single item of men's clothing, his eyebrows plucked and all body hair removed, he was an example of the homosexual whores Father Ritter had described.

I knew few people realized how often boys were forced to prostitute themselves to older homosexuals. Even I, a policeman, was not aware that the gaming process and control by fear was as common in the gay community as in the heterosexual vice world.

Clarence, the female impersonator, had come to Midwest Challenge and Safe House through a local church where he'd found the first real joy in his life.

"Jesus Christ," he told me in a voice still reeking with gay inflections.

But he *was* born again. He was trying to

discard the past. He wanted a change to men's clothing and a chance to learn more about the Christian lifestyle.

"To be a man," he said slowly in a lower tone.

"You'll have that chance," I promised.

One of my staff wondered where Clarence was supposed to live.

"Certainly not with the girls at Safe House. This isn't that kind of rehabilitation program," said another, a flash of mirth crossing his face.

I started to tell him to be serious, but figured God allowed a little honest and harmless levity in such otherwise trying circumstances. Perhaps it could be called a safety valve for Christians under pressure.

Clarence moved in with men completing phase two of the Midwest Challenge program. They were glad to help him learn to live as a Christian. He talked of little else. He quickly became a devout Bible student. Whenever I asked how he'd become a male prostitute, he quoted the scriptures. So many scriptures that I knew he was trying to hide something.

He finally told me, "I was raised by the high priest and priestess of a satanic cult. I've been a devil worshiper too."

We prayed together that he'd never see another devil. Later, I prayed alone: "Lord, give me the strength and wisdom to succeed at the many tasks you've given me to perform."

All the television networks and many large newspapers joined *Time, Newsweek* and *People* magazines in contacting me. They wanted to know if my trip had been successful, and what my plans were for the future. Encouraging them to run stories, I told everything except my plans to return to New York City. Publicity was a great help, but next time I'd decided to sneak into town and surprise the pimps. Afterward, breaking a success story, I hoped to attract more attention and more girls.

Almost every Sunday and occasionally during the week, I spoke at churches across Minnesota, Iowa and Wisconsin. Requests for my talks increased tremendously as stories about my work began appearing in national magazines. I added new topics, emphasizing the role of parents in the prevention of prostitution.

"There are three effective ways to reduce, if not stop, prostitution," I told my audiences. "The enforcement of new and stricter laws that provide stern punishment for pimps and the men that hire their whores. The establishment of alternative lifestyles for prostitutes through facilities like Safe House. And, most important, the education of parents."

They had to learn to give and receive love. Love was the key to their daughters' salvation. Without it, many girls would end up on the Minnesota Strip or some other street to hell.

I began taking Lynn and Elaine with me to give terrifying testimony of what prostitutes endured, witness to their wonderful new lives with Christ, and explain what I meant about parents.

Audiences cried when Lynn described the way her father used her emotions like a ping-pong ball giving, giving, giving material things but making her repay him by never asking for love.

He built her up, up, up when she put him in a good mood by pretending no need for his time or attention. He drove her down, reminding her that she'd become a worthless toy to be discarded after her cute baby days, whenever she got in the way of his personal interests.

"Don't play games with your kids," she begged.

They were angry when they heard about pimps torturing the girls, crying again when they learned those same pimps had become distorted father symbols—protectors, guardians and lovers to fatherless girls who had lived in homes that were only cold and empty shells.

141

"Yes, that's where it all begins," I often said. "In cold and empty shells."

Usually, toward the end of the program, one of the girls would begin a prayer.

"Thank you, Jesus, for helping me to find a safe and useful place . . ."

Other girls began getting the message. Calls came in from prostitutes across the country. Most refused to give their names or talk about themselves. They only wanted to know if Safe House was "for real." None had called back yet.

"But it's only a matter of time," I told my wife, Gayle, as I rushed in for Thanksgiving dinner. "After the next trip to New York I think Safe House is going to begin filling up."

Chapter 14

Christmas, always a joyful time, brought me a few hours of especially welcomed rest. During the previous month I'd been rushing constantly, trying to divide my time between regular police work, administration of Midwest Challenge, supervision of Safe House, fund raising, speaking engagements, continuing investigations of prostitution, interviews with prospects for my programs, and secret preparations for the next trip to New York City.

With the approval of the mayor and the police chief of Minneapolis, I was flying east in the morning. Eleven people from the Midwest Challenge and Safe House programs were driving vans loaded with inspirational material and small yellow cards printed with a "Hotline to Freedom, 1-612-825-2469 (call collect 24 hours)," and a message: "Are you hassled by your pimp? And are you ready to make a change in your life? We offer protection. And transportation to a 'Safe House' in Minneapolis. Safe House is the first of its kind—a Christ-centered program offering understanding, training, help and direction for a new life. It's free. Call us if you're serious. We care."

The young people accompanying me would stay at Teen Challenge headquarters in Brooklyn where Randy Larson, an old buddy from my Bible school days, was assistant director. He endorsed my plans, believing help for prostitutes was as important as helping drug addicts. As far as I was concerned prostitutes were also addicted—to their pimps.

A lady cop accompanied me to help supervise and protect the young people, especially the girls who were subject to the fear syndrome and obvious targets for the pimps. The New York detectives assigned to Select Committee on Crime were to meet and assist us.

The trip had been kept secret, with only the Minneapolis authorities and the Select Committee on Crime knowing my plans. I didn't want word to leak and warn the pimps and vice lords.

On the morning of December 27, 1977, before I led my group to the filthy sidewalks of the Minnesota Strip, I read from the Bible II Timothy 1:7: "For God hath not given us the spirit of fear; but of power, and of love, and of a sound mind."

We needed that. It reminded us all that, like Elaine, God had plans for us. We prayed we'd begin to make those plans work.

As we arrived on 8th Avenue, I noticed the crowds were thinner than usual. Few hookers were visible. I soon saw why. New York police department paddy wagons and squad cars were everywhere. A large force of law enforcement officers was sweeping the prostitutes off the Minnesota Strip.

Had the publicity generated the month before prodded the administration into positive action? I doubted it. Prostitutes were being rounded up so my group couldn't talk to them. Apparently someone had tipped off corrupt officials who feared I'd convince too many talkative girls to return to Minneapolis with me. If I succeeded to prove and break the Minnesota connection with their testimony, New York City's administration would suffer further embarrassment, the pimps and the revenue they generated would disappear, conventioneers and thrill-seeking tourists would lose opportunities to play dirty games away from home, and many vulnerable bigshots would spend sleepless nights.

I slammed my fist into the palm of the other hand. Cronies of the vice lords were depriving the girls on the Minnesota Strip of a chance to salvage their minds, bodies and souls.

"There's nothing you can do about it," said a detective. "The N.Y.P.D. is simply following orders to enforce the law."

"Just like during the Tammany days," I growled as I climbed out of the van. "Well, I don't give a damn what they're pretending to do, we're going to try to find some girls in spite of this rotten interference."

We got to a few girls before they were hustled away. None would listen to us for long. All were terribly hostile. They seemed to be more afraid of a smiling community relations officer and a group of friendly youngsters than of the hard-faced cops shoving them into barred vehicles. One said she hated *all* cops. "I wouldn't want one to come to help me even if I was being raped. He'd just take over."

Another would only say "shit," even when I promised she could save herself with a nod.

Elaine found a girl whose face was swollen to a reddened pulp nearly twice normal size. The girl ran as I approached.

"She thought you looked like the john who did that to her," said Elaine, reminding me that pimps weren't the only men using violence. Some johns felt safe assaulting hookers, even on the street in broad daylight, because they figured the law would never interfere.

Late in the day, I finally found a girl who pretended to listen. Toward the end of my description of the Safe House program, she interrupted.

"What about money?"

"All allowance to begin with, later wages."

She frowned. "And fun."

I described our recreational activities and, thinking she might once have wanted to be a singer, told about the Midwest Challenge choir. "They're really popular. They travel all over."

"How? In handcuffs?" she hollered, giving me the finger and turning to jog toward a pimp rounding the corner.

The policeman at the intersection chuckled. When I started to follow the girl, he called to me, "Give up."

Coming to tell me the group was about to move farther down the Strip, Lynn overheard. For a moment I thought she was going to give the New York policeman the finger. She stared at him instead.

"Pig."

I motioned her to take it easy. "Any incidents with the New York police will only make our job harder."

Lynn was silent as we hurried to catch up with our group. Just before we reached them she tugged at my arm. I stopped to see what she wanted.

"I haven't lost hope. We'll get some of the girls to come to Safe House. But listen, Al, don't expect any help from the New York cops. Just the opposite. Like I told you a long time ago, there's some pretty heavy dudes fooling around with prostitutes. The cops have to protect 'em. Wait 'til you see my diary." She moved close to me and whispered. "When I was being passed around among big business executives and politicians I heard one girl brag that she'd turned a trick with a Vice President of the United States. And you've read about Frank Sinatra's friend, Judy Exner. She was with John F. Kennedy."

She kept talking. Angry and vindictive because of the way the authorities were treating us, her memory improved. Much of what I'd been waiting patiently to read in her diary came out now. Most sounded true, but I knew it would be nearly impossible for me to prove.

"As soon as you think it's safe we've got to get that diary to the F.B.I.," I said softly.

"It's about time vice got yanked out of the closets in the ivory towers."

"You know I'll help anyway I can." Lynn's eyes darted between mine and approaching pedestrians. "But not here. Later in Minneapolis."

She rushed ahead of me down 8th Avenue, giving out the yellow cards to anyone who passed. She even stopped cops who were still looking for stray hookers. If I hadn't followed her closely and been ready to intercede, Lynn would have been arrested herself.

"She was soliciting me," insisted the burly officer pulling her toward an unmarked car.

I identified myself and asked him to read the yellow card.

"Crap," he said, releasing Lynn and tossing our message into the gutter.

"There's another so-called policeman who deserves to be called 'pig,'" Lynn muttered as he sauntered away.

I didn't sleep much that night. I got up to pray many times. When the detectives assigned to help me arrived in the morning, they suggested that I try other areas frequented by prostitutes. Not wanting to lead my youngsters into stranger territory yet, I went with them alone. Lexington Avenue and 86th Street was usually as busy a corner as any on the Minnesota Strip, they said.

That day, it too was nearly void of hookers. It was the same wherever we went. The detectives showed me hotels where Minnesota teenagers lived with their pimps and others that were used for tricking. I recognized many names from the lists Lynn had given me.

"Why don't you raid them?" I asked, then signalled that they needn't reply. I already knew the answer.

After lunch I decided to strike out on my own. I found a sympathetic cab driver who took me to places where "classier girls" hung out. Several were standing by the bar at P.J. Clark's on 2nd Avenue, but they didn't look any classier than the girls on the Minnesota Strip.

"I guess you're right," said the cab driver. "In that kind of business it doesn't take long for a girl to look like hell. It's a terrible life, especially along 8th Avenue. Dangerous too."

As he whipped his cab through traffic, he described a girl who'd been murdered by her pimp the previous August. She was pushed from a tenth-floor window in a dingy hotel off Times Square.

I shuddered. It could have been Candy.

Approaching the corner of 8th Avenue and 42nd Street, the driver began shaking his finger toward the windshield. "If there was a way to stop the hooking this'd be the place to start. But there's no way because the law's behind the whole rotten business."

When he turned to tell me the fare I saw his expression was as sour as a man swallowing his own vomit.

My spirits improved when Lynn and Elaine reported a few hookers were returning to the Minnesota Strip. None would spend much time talking but quite a few were taking the yellow card to pass around.

Probably alerted by the uncommon police activity in the vice districts, the press discovered I'd returned. There being no further benefits in secrecy and great possible value in publicity, I answered their questions.

"No, we haven't found any girls to go back to Minneapolis with us."

"Yes, we are distributing stacks of literature, Christian literature, and spreading words of the Safe House program to everyone we can find on the Minnesota Strip."

"Why don't you ask the local police where all the girls have gone?"

After another day of many frustrations it was time to leave New York City. Again I was returning without any girls. But, as before, not emptyhanded. Publicity exposing the Minnesota Strip, the widespread vice and corruption it represented, and the hostile attitude of the city government was mounting. The Minnesota connection was becoming an issue. I wondered how soon President Carter, who was promising to expend a lot of national energy promoting human rights around the world, would begin giving some attention to the real victims of "victimless crimes" in the United States.

I had more detailed information than ever before. Though representatives of the Select Committee on Crime may have leaked the story of my visit, many of their investigative files had been made available. With the additional answers I knew I could find in Minneapolis the riddle of the Minnesota connection seemed ready to be solved. I found myself humming a hymn on the way to the airport.

An unhappy surprise dampened my enthusiasm as I was waiting for the plane. I was advised that the two detectives who'd been helping me were being reassigned—away from the Select Committee, away from the nosey Minneapolis preacher-cop, away from the vice rackets.

Pressure from eastern political and business sources began soon after I arrived home. I ignored it. Albert Hofstede, the newly elected mayor of Minneapolis, stood up to it, saying his city had "moral fiber." Though he and Elmer Nordlund, the new chief of police, discouraged my return to New York in the near future—"If the pipeline begins here, this is the best place to turn off the valve"—they encouraged the speedy development of the Safe House program to its fullest potential.

When an anonymous caller asked me if my "crazy crusade" was ending, the words of John Paul Jones seemed the most appropriate answer: "I've just begun to fight."

The publicity and the calls made my wife nervous. She wondered where it was all going to end. Her serenity returned when I reminded her God had a plan for everything. Certainly there'd been failures and negative reactions. But there were many positives too. The phones at Safe House were ringing constantly. Girls wanted help. Public-spirited citizens offered donations to expand the program. Police officers volunteered their time and effort.

Ginger was nearly ready to support herself with honest work, establish a household and reclaim her child. Lynn and Elaine had become my working partners, joining me in most speaking engagements and appearing with me on television programs. Clarence looked, walked and talked like a Christian man. And, because he'd FOUND IT, he was.

They were all learning to know Jesus Christ in a much deeper way than any had ever thought possible.

Safe House was filling up. There'd have to

be another soon, and another. So many girls and boys were still suffering on the sin-soaked streets and in the dens of the vice lords. Somewhere among them, if she were still alive, was Candy. And the Ellens, Barbaras, Graces, Cheryls ...

Epilogue

Could the Minnesota connection be broken, the pipeline shut off? I believed it could. So did Mayor Hofstede and Chief Nordlund. A new police task force was formed to fight prostitution, especially juvenile prostitution, in Minneapolis.

The Mayor said, "Police departments may change, improve, adjust to the times. I want to see our law enforcement officers working with the community which, though it has a strong religious base, cannot hope to legislate morality. To build moral fiber, you have to get out among the people and talk about what's right and wrong. Then everyone must try to improve our society. If a city loses its will to solve problems, to stay alive, it dies."

He felt very strongly that there were more than enough people in Minneapolis with a will to solve problems. The adverse publicity accompanying any vice-related story did not scare him because *his* city was going to do something about it.

Chief Nordlund was determined to help with the housecleaning. "We're going to make Minneapolis a very unhappy home-town for pimps and an equally unpleasant place for them to visit."

Most of my fellow police officers were supportive, though some kidded me about the publicity my program was receiving. "You're already a preacher and a cop. What's next, television stardom?"

They were referring to my appearance on the Phil Donahue show when two of the ex-prostitutes and I had described the Minnesota connection. During the question period a lady in the audience had asked one of the girls if she'd ever undergone intense psychoanalysis. My reaction was pretty strong—"A hard act to follow," someone said. I'd told the lady that girls living as prostitutes needed something to motivate a fast change of mind and lifestyle, not a rehash of a rotten childhood. When I'd asked the rest of the audience if they agreed there was a resounding "yes."

I expanded the theme on the P.T.L. Club

television program. The prime motivator was Jesus Christ. He was helping make the Safe House program work.

During the first three months of 1978, 12 girls left the Minnesota Strip and returned to Minneapolis. They were in hiding, reorganizing their lives. Soon they'd begin giving me information to help more like them escape a life of prostitution.

The public everywhere began demanding action. And crackdowns weren't only against prostitutes as in the past. Representative Frederick W. Richmond of Brooklyn was arrested for soliciting an undercover police officer for prostitution on April 6, 1978.

"Yes," I said, "now they're going to rattle a lot of dirty skeletons in the closets of the ivory towers."

Lynn retrieved her diary and several weeks later the FBI entered the case she was making against corporate prostitution.

At 3:30 p.m. on Thursday, April 25, 1978, I led a caravan of police cars and Midwest Challenge vans to the entrance of Crystal Court in the IDS building. With the support of the city administration and the police department, Minneapolis law enforcement officers joined young people from Midwest Challenge and Safe House in a mass effort to save teenage girls from the horrors of a life of prostitution. Their pimps scattered when they saw us coming. We found many girls beginning or about to begin playing their vicious game. One 17-year-old, already an "old-timer," asked to come away with us immediately.

"I admit I'm a whore, but I've got to find something better. Please . . ." She took a deep breath, dried a tear, and stepped into one of the vans.

"Rest and be peaceful. Listen, while I tell you how I began a new life." A girl from Safe House reached out to her, smiling.

The next evening I was working in my office when the Hotline to Freedom rang. I answered quickly, as I always did, hoping it would be a very special call.

"Do you think you can help me? I'm pretty bad," said a sorrowful voice. "I'm hiding from my pimp right now, but maybe I should go back to him. Like I said, I'm pretty bad. Nobody else is going to want me."

I began to pray silently but very hard. I wanted the youngster to reveal her hiding place so I could rush to show her someone did care. When I heard tears in her voice, I began to cry. As had many voices during the last ten months, this one sounded like Candy's.

THE BEST OF THE BESTSELLERS
FROM WARNER BOOKS!

DAUGHTERS OF THE WILD COUNTRY   (82-583, $2.25)
by Aola Vandergriff
THE DAUGHTERS OF THE SOUTHWIND travel northward to the wild country of Russian Alaska, where nature is raw, men are rough, and love, when it comes, shines like a gold nugget in the cold Alaskan waters. A lusty sequel to a giant bestseller.

THE FRENCH ATLANTIC AFFAIR   (81-562, $2.50)
by Ernest Lehman
In mid-ocean, the S.S. Marseille is taken over! The conspirators—174 of them—are unidentifiable among the other passengers. Unless a ransom of 35 million dollars in gold is paid within 48 hours, the ship and everyone on it will be blown skyhigh!

DARE TO LOVE by Jennifer Wilde   (81-826, $2.50)
Who dared to love Elena Lopez? Who was willing to risk reputation and wealth to win the Spanish dancer who was the scandal of Europe? Kings, princes, great composers and writers . . . the famous and wealthy men of the 19th century vied for her affection, fought duels for her.

THE OTHER SIDE OF THE MOUNTAIN:
PART 2 by E.G. Valens   (82-463, $2.25)
Part 2 of the inspirational story of a young Olympic contender's courageous climb from paralysis and total helplessness to a useful life and meaningful marriage. An NBC-TV movie and serialized in **Family Circle** magazine.

THE KINGDOM by Ronald Joseph   (81-467, $2.50)
The saga of a passionate and powerful family who carves out of the wilderness the largest cattle ranch in the world. Filled with both adventure and romance, hard-bitten empire building and tender moments of intimate love, **The Kingdom** is a book for all readers.

THE GREEK TYCOON by Eileen Lottman   (82-712, $2.25)
The story of a romance that fascinated the world—between the mightiest magnate on earth and the woman he loved . . . the woman who would become the widow of the President of the United States.

THE BEST OF THE BESTSELLERS
FROM WARNER BOOKS!